ARE YOU
PSYCHIC?

DOROTHY CHITTY

ARE YOU
PSYCHIC ?

BARNES
& NOBLE

NEW YORK

This edition published by Barnes & Noble Publishing, Inc.,
by arrangement with HarperElement,
an imprint of HarperCollins*Publishers*

2005 Barnes & Noble Books

M 10 9 8 7 6 5 4 3 2 1

ISBN 0-7607-7473-0

Printed and bound in China by
Imago

Contents

The Exercises

Chapter 1 – Awakening Sensitivity

Chapter 2 – Meeting Spirit Guides

Chapter 3 – Spirit Readings

Chapter 4 – Soul Healing

Chapter 5 – Past Lives

Chapter 6 – Talking with Animals

I dedicate this book to my husband Michael, my fellow traveller along this path of discovery, whose loving suport has made my personal journey possible.

Acknowledgements

I would like to thank the following people, who in their own special way have helped me to stay focused on this book.

Jackie McCorkindale, for spending many hours gleaning information from me and for transcribing the original work; Ian McCorkindale, for his help in computing the same to Michele; Michele Pilley, who was instrumental in the promotion and acceptance of this project and for her professional guidance into the world of publishing; Belinda Budge, my unsung hero, for her unwavering support and belief in me and this book throughout; Katy Carrington, my editor, and the staff at ThorsonsElement who have worked diligently on my behalf; Liz Dean whose expertise and spiritual depth helped to reshape the final draft.

To my family, for their humorous understanding of their somewhat weird, but always loving, mother, mother-in-law, grandmother, sister, sister-in-law, auntie 'D' and wife.

Last, but not least, my gratitude to my many friends, too numerous to mention, for the support and encouragement that they have given me through the years.

Foreword

As a child, 'God' was my name for my main spirit guide. He always appeared in a suit of rough, brown cloth and I thought the fact that God wore a brown suit quite normal, really. He held my hand, right through school, and I could see and hear him. When I got older I met new spirit guides, and God didn't come so often. I now see that God had been a monk – which may have explained why he was so good at helping me with Latin translation.

I had other guides, too, all of whom were my friends. As a child, I never thought that they had lived or died, and never questioned why I would know what may happen to some people in the future, or why someone was ill. Today, I often refer to my guides as 'my friends' or 'Spirit'. I have always accepted them, and the way in which they work with me during a reading. But I would never take it for granted. I am excited about what I do, because my work is about talking to people. We all have the potential to be the best we can be, and through working with Spirit I hope that I help people to find their path in life, to heal the past, to feel the love of those they have lost in this life. You too have spirit guides. In reading this book, you have taken the first step towards meeting them.

I'm an ordinary woman. I don't intellectualise what I do, but I have extraordinary conversations with the deceased and the living. In part, this book is about my personal voyage of discovery as I have learned to develop and harness my sensitive skills; my dialogue with Spirit. I communicate with my spirit guides every day, and with people in spirit who come to talk to their loved ones. I also talk with those who cannot speak in a way that others can understand, such as babies in the womb, and children with disabilities that prevent them talking. I also speak with animals. If you think this sounds too far-fetched, I would like to tell you that all I need to communicate as a sensitive, or medium, are my senses. Everyone has senses, and the potential for sensitivity.

Developing your sensitivity

You may not see spirits yet, or hear them talk to you, but this doesn't mean that you are not sensitive. We all have the potential to be receptive to other energies and beings, and learn to communicate with them. Because we are all different, we experience this contact in different ways, but always through the senses – our heart and soul, not our heads. If Spirit want to talk to you, they will do it in a way that you can recognise. Knowing when this is happening takes awareness and practice. How often have you thought, 'I knew that would happen', after a particular occurrence? How many times have you been thinking of someone, only to find that the very same person phones, writes, or you both meet unexpectedly? How many times have you had a good – or not so good – feeling about someone, and then discover later that your feelings were justified? These are some of the clues being impressed upon you to let you know that you have more help at hand than you could imagine. This is the sensitive psychic in you, awaiting acknowledgement. When you follow these inner urges, it often means that you are listening to spirit without realising. Using this book will teach you how to understand and utilise your inner knowledge by connecting with your guide – a loved one or a dear friend in Spirit who has come to help you.

In order to begin the process of opening up your innate sensitive ability, you simply need to acknowledge the souls of your departed loved ones, known to you either in this life or in past lives. They come in love, and love only. In order to acknowledge them, all you need to do is say, 'Welcome, come closer', and you will get a sense of who they are.

Throughout this book, I have set down the exercises which I use in the sensitivity workshops that I run. These exercises were given to me by my spirit guides, who continue to be my greatest teachers. If followed correctly, together these exercises form a comprehensive blueprint for developing your sensitivity, exploring your chakras and meeting your spirit guides. This will enable you to recognise the spiritual truths that are at the very foundation of your being, so allowing you to access healing for yourself and others. In addition, the way will be open for you to reach into memories of past lives, so providing a deeper understanding of why you behave as you do. Lastly, we explore the rewarding but little known area of communicating with animals and I will teach you techniques which will enable you to develop this skill.

Over many years as a working sensitive, I have read for thousands of clients, and many have chosen to develop their own sensitivity. Some people simply want to make sense of their own experiences while others wish go on to use their sensitivity to help others. I hope that through describing my journey as a sensitive, and my workshop exercises, it will inspire you all to develop the sensitivity with which you were born and help enrich your lives.

Chapter 1

Awakening Sensitivity

I was ten years old, and about to be assessed by a psychiatrist. I didn't know what a psychiatrist was; as far as I understood, I was going to see a doctor. I was there in his office with my parents, at the request of my teachers – I had been in trouble at school.

He asked one question after another, and I answered without worrying too much about what I was saying. I don't remember any of the questions now. After a while, he turned to my parents and concluded: 'She's strongly borderline.' I had no idea what 'borderline' meant. He was simply addressing my parents and dismissing me.

It was then I saw a small boy standing next to the psychiatrist, right by his desk. He was maybe five or six years old. Through my mind he told me that his name was Peter. Peter said, 'That's my dad!' He asked me to tell his dad that he was there.

Allowing Peter to speak through me, I said, 'I'm Peter, and I've come to talk to you.' The doctor stared down at me. 'Your little boy Peter's here, and he wants to talk to you.'

'No, he's not,' he retorted.

'Yes, I am,' said the little boy. Then Peter told me how he died – from leukaemia – and that his father had placed a special toy in his coffin. His mother hadn't known about it. This is exactly what I told his father.

The doctor then started to ask Peter questions through me. We began to have a three-way conversation. This seemed entirely natural at the time, although in retrospect it must have been a very emotional experience for both father and his son.

Afterwards, the doctor spoke to my parents again. 'There's nothing wrong with your daughter,' he concluded. 'She's got ESP, and a vivid imagination.' That's the first time that I had heard that term and I kept asking my dad, 'What's ESP? Is it catching?' My dad told me that it just meant I was a bit different.

Looking back, I can see that the psychiatrist I saw was remarkably enlightened, especially considering the medical profession's scepticism of ESP in the 1950s. I also feel that because this psychiatrist had lost his son, his trauma allowed him to be sensitive towards me. Nowadays I work with many bereaved parents, and I know that they always want their children to be safe in the spirit world. I remember seeing the psychiatrist's face when I was channelling his son Peter, and I had a strong feeling that this big man was close to tears. In the event, he didn't dissolve, but I had a sense that his emotions were very close to the surface.

I now know that Spirit were giving me validation – information so specific to the psychiatrist that he could be in no doubt that the messages were genuine. If Peter hadn't come into the meeting, I don't know what would have happened to me. But because I escaped stigma, my world of spirits stayed intact.

My earliest spiritual memories are of my spirit friends, or, as I later realised, my spirit guides. To me, they were ordinary men and women whom I talked with incessantly, just as I would with anyone else in my family. They were with me always, chatting to me at home and in school. These conversations felt so instinctive to me that I accepted their presence completely. I knew that these beings were different from the living people around me, but I assumed that everyone else was able to see and hear their own friends in spirit walking alongside them, just as I did.

In my early years, my best spirit friend – who I called 'God' – was my constant companion. I played truant from school with him, nipping off to the park to play on the swings. We'd go to the roundabout, and he would lift me onto it and spin it around with me holding on tightly until I was dizzy with excitement. God's invisibility didn't really register until one day we walked past the sweet shop together. He was holding my hand, as he always did, and I wanted to look in the shop window. We turned, and I saw myself, but God wasn't there. I could feel his hand in mine. I could hear him. I could feel him. I could see him standing next to me if I turned – but he had no reflection! I can still recall the feelings of shock and wonder as I gazed at the glass of the window, not understanding why I couldn't see God.

At school – a Catholic girls' school – I was constantly in trouble for talking back to the nuns. If a teacher explained a point of theology to the class, I would invariably contradict her – I couldn't help but say something. This was principally because

I talked to my spirit guides and they taught me about all sorts of things, although I was never given any information to help with my homework or in exams. I wasn't academically competitive, but I stuck out as being a know-all, which meant that I sometimes felt excluded from the other children – the other girls all thought that I was very opinionated. But, just as my conversations with my spirit friends exposed my difference, so in time they helped me to become accepted by the other girls.

One day, some of my classmates were playing skipping in the playground. I loved skipping and wanted to join in with them, but I knew they didn't want me to. I hung around, waiting for an opportunity to creep in and take my turn. I saw a chance, ran under the rope and started skipping. The other girls began to taunt me, and then one of them hit me. The game stopped and the others joined in, shouting and thumping me. I fought back as hard as I could and then suddenly I heard my spirit friend God talking to me.

'It's not the answer,' he chided.

'God, what do you want me to do?' I asked. All the other girls looked at me and I realised I had been talking out loud. I don't know if they heard what

I had said, but maybe they sensed that something important was happening. God said, 'Tell them that you would like to play with them their way.'

So I turned to the girls and asked, 'Can I play with you? Can I play skipping your way?'

Incredibly, the girl leading the game looked at me and reluctantly replied: 'Yes, all right. You can join us.'

From that moment, they accepted me. They probably thought I was a bit strange, but maybe they also knew that I could be good fun, too. With God by my side, I always felt that I could be brave in moments of adversity, and that I would have the confidence to stand up to people.

My teachers, however, were less accepting of my behaviour. I had gained a reputation for daydreaming, insubordination, telling lies and playing truant: overall, my teachers suspected that I had a problem with reality. It was because of this that the school had requested that my parents take me to a psychiatrist, which led to my extrasensory abilities being recognised.

My mother had always been my confidant and I talked to her about God and my other spirit friends.

She was psychic too, and often read tea leaves. After I had been 'diagnosed' with ESP (and not a mental illness, to my mother's relief) my sensitivity had a name, but my mother asked me not to talk about it to others. She did not want me labelled or ostracised. Her protectiveness was understandable given the experiences of her sister, my aunt Lottie. Lottie had similar abilities to me and talked to her guides openly. This was in the 1950s and in those days people who talked to 'themselves' were seen as exhibiting signs of mental illness. Because of this, for a short period, Lottie had been placed in a mental institution. I had seen Lottie's guides myself, and when I had told her this she was horrified and asked me to keep quiet for my own sake. Perhaps because of the pressure to conform, I'm ashamed to say that I didn't want Spirit around me much at that point in my life, either. So I kept my sensitivity secret for a time. But it has always been there – it's who I am, and how I see the world.

I've been called a psychic and medium, but a 'sensitive' more accurately describes my nature and what I do. For me, sensitivity is about 'Spirit' talking to me through my senses. I use my sense-itivity to tune in to energy. I think of this as conversing with Spirit, or my spirit guides, whom I hear, see, smell and feel every day. As I talk with my clients, I listen to Spirit.

Spirit teaches me, and through Spirit, I communicate with those who have passed over, and with those still living.

The 'Gift'

Many people assume that to be psychic, or sensitive, is a gift at birth – you either have it, or you don't – but this isn't the case at all. Although I have naturally communicated with Spirit all my life – for more than fifty years now – but I have still had to learn a great deal along the way. Developing sensitivity is something that is open to everyone. It is simply a matter of learning to recognise your senses at work, and fine-tuning them to revitalise the connection between you and the other energies around you. I believe that when you reactivate your senses, you then become open to higher communication. You become sensitive, and live sensationally again.

We are all born with heightened sensitivity but most people become closed off from this as they grow older. As children, we are open to imaginative adventures and invisible friends; we often love nature and are fascinated by animals. Some children, as I did, are able to see Spirit, but we all experience amazing sensitivity when we are small. In fact, children see Spirit more than we realise, because they are so much more open and accepting. Often a child will say something that seems beyond their age and comprehension. What is really happening is that they are repeating information they have received from Spirit. This may also be coupled with the child's ability to recall ancient memories. If asked, sometimes a child will talk to an adult about their 'invisible' friends. If they do, never ridicule them as it will make them feel slighted and stupid – and it may close a beautiful world to them. When she was little, my daughter, Tanya, had a spirit friend called Emma, who came with her little dog, Toby. If we were going out in the car together, I would make sure I left the car door open for a few moments after Tanya had got in to make sure there was time for Emma and Toby to climb into the back seat with her. I encouraged and accepted Emma and Toby in our lives, and I believe that if children are supported to enjoy their relationships with their friends in spirit, they will grow up to be caring adults, sensitive to the world around them. After all, children are the future and they may grow up to bring wonderful changes to the world.

I hope this doesn't sound too serious. Psychic ability doesn't require gravitas – although I take what I do seriously, I don't take myself seriously.

It's an important distinction, because with sensitivity comes responsibility and joy. Expanding your senses means you can enjoy your experience of life all the more. At one point I went through a phase of wanting to be perfect in some way and I began to take myself very seriously; some might call this a sense of humour failure, which to a degree it was. Through this I learned that I didn't have to live in an austere way in order to be spiritual. My humour is an important aspect of the way I communicate – my guides often laugh with me, like friends. Living with sensitivity is about being who you are now.

Sensitivity sabotage

Our sensitivity may lay dormant for years due to the work we do, the relationships we form or the general pattern of our life experience. Our reconnection with Spirit – our essence – may be subtle or dramatic, and it may come at any time of life, from our twenties to our seventies and beyond. What matters is that reconnecting with Spirit puts us back in touch with the truth of who we are.

I know that traumatic experiences can appear to sabotage happiness. Like many people, at one time or another I have suffered the loss of someone very close to me, illness and financial crisis. Yet the way we have lived prior to such an event may have been sabotaging our sensitivity and true life path. In some cases, trauma is the only way that Spirit – the energies that psychics work with – can get our attention. We receive a wake-up call that transforms our lives.

Many people have their first experience of Spirit when someone they love dies. For the first time, we may hear a friend say that they are sure that their loved partner or relative is close by. They are sensitive to the signs around them. A client of mine experienced her sensitivity only after the death of her sister, feeling her presence for days after the funeral. It is important to understand that when someone dies or we experience trauma, Spirit are not punishing us, or exacting a price for sensitivity – they are just trying to tell us that the life path we've travelled up to that point now needs to change.

In my experience, trauma often coincides with increased sensitivity in other areas of life, because it can act as a trigger to put us back in touch with who we are. Many clients of mine, whether bereaved or reeling from the shock of redundancy or a relationship break-up, have told me how they had begun to 'sense' a place before visiting it. One client recalled seeing the trees in the garden and the layout of the living room of his daughter's new house, weeks before he visited her. Such experiences can feel confusing for people who have been unused to taking notice of their senses. Yet this is the language of sensitivity. For instance, I know that a tingling sensation on my temple tells me a particular guide is talking to me – their way. When I can smell roses, I know my mother is sitting next to me.

All too often, I hear people putting these experiences down to being out of sorts, or worse, being oversensitive. The word sensitive has become virtual criticism – a sensitive child is a 'problem' or 'difficult' – and this may give us the message that it's not safe to have finer feelings.

As adults, we often repress our senses because of the environment in which we live. We expend energy trying to block out the noise from traffic and neighbours; we learn how to develop a blind spot for the unsightly or disturbing; sometimes we wish ourselves invisible in the press of a crowd. We want to sense less, not more, because peace and quiet can feel such scarce commodities. But, just as you have chosen to suppress sensitivity, so you can choose to regain it. It's a choice you can make. Your senses are your spiritual connectors, through which you can live a sensitive and spiritual existence.

I have found that many people who have burgeoning psychic ability may want to ignore it, particularly if they are surrounded by friends and family who do not accept their sensitivity. At the heart of this is the fear of being labelled as a bit odd. Given that many children and adults resist being 'different', it's not surprising that we try to suppress our sensitivity before someone notices that we don't fit in.

Total sensation

Sensitivity is about using all the senses together. When Spirit communicate with me, I may hear them as sound, feel their presence as vibration in my body or sense them as colour in my peripheral vision. Because all my senses are heightened, Spirit can always find a way to talk with me. This is my personal definition of ESP: the cumulative effect of all five heightened senses working together to enable a 'sixth sense'. Although the dictionary may define ESP as means of 'obtaining information about the environment without the use of normal sensory channels', in my experience, ESP doesn't just come from nowhere. Psychic ability, or sensitivity, relies upon us using our everyday senses in every possible way.

Several years ago, I was fortunate enough to see an opera singer rehearsing her scales before a performance. I say 'saw' rather than 'heard', because I realised I was able to see the energy coming from her mouth as she sang. It was the colour of purple velvet. She had the most beautiful voice, and it was all the more magnificent because I could see and hear it.

The next time I experienced the sight of music was as the Glyndebourne Festival. Watching several performers sing together, again I could see the colour of a voice, but this time it was even more spectacular. I saw the energy pouring out of the singers' mouths – the tenors were purple, the sopranos indigo; others were shades of mauve and some even yellow. And I could sense how the singers put themselves behind the high notes. When a long note resonated, I could see the tremor in the colour.

I have never understood why I saw those colours. Maybe it was because I could truly feel the music – the sound resonated so deeply within me that I was literally shown the beauty of music through colour. Looking back, I realise that sometimes I was seeing the colour of the sound before the sound itself, perhaps because light travels faster than sound. Psychic phenomena and modern physics may have more in common than we think!

Some of you may be able to see sound as colour as I do. When you next hear live music, try feeling the colours. You may see a faint aura of colour around a musician, or the colour of a note. Try half-closing your eyes and relax your mental focus – when you do this, sensitivity can come in unawares (see page 30 for more on seeing with peripheral vision).

Sensitive situations

We are often most in touch with our sensitivity when we are in emotional situations. If we feel deep compassion for another person, we can really sense their energy. When we fall in love, our energy is revitalised as our senses heighten. We feel temperature more keenly, and our sense of smell is often heightened. I do sense Spirit through smell at times, but more commonly I experience dramatic changes in temperature when I am reading for people. I get really hot, then I can become cold and, when Spirit come in, I can be really freezing. It is a particular, unusual kind of cold, which I've become used to recognising. When I am working with a client, Spirit just pour energy through me and, if I need to send a healing thought to someone, that heat comes through. Again, through years of practice I have learned to recognise this as the presence of Spirit.

Often I find that it is the simple day-to-day experiences that bring me sensory gifts – from the sound of the rain to the mist in my garden, anything that is beautiful can massage my senses back to life, even when I'm feeling tired. In the same way, when you are not feeling tuned-in or at home with yourself, it can be revitalising to remember your sensitive experiences. You can also practice the Centring exercise (*see* page 32) to help ground you when life feels frenetic. It's important to understand that developing your sensitivity can mean being more sensitive to your own needs as well as those of others.

My sensitivity gives me information about other people. I try not to judge what I sense; I simply register it for what it is – information. As well as listening to Spirit, I pick up information from a person's emotional body, or energy – we all do this, and usually call it 'instinct'. More precisely, this is soul knowledge at work, with one soul picking up information from another without conscious awareness. It explains why we may take an instant like or dislike to someone. In a positive sense, we often express this as 'love at first sight'.

I usually sense passionate emotion visually and vibrationally. When I am in a room with someone who is angry for example, I experience their emotions as shards of glass pricking my body, and sometimes I'll see intense colour around them. If I encounter someone who has just had an argument, their energy feels spiky. Sadness always feels heavy, and looks grey. And if someone unconsciously enjoys being a depressive, you can feel them for a long time after you've been in their company. They stay connected to you out of their own need – unknowingly, they have become energy leeches. In the past I have experienced this simply by thinking about them and feeling my energy levels drop. So, honing your senses can help you tell the difference between someone who is habitually down, and a person who is reacting to difficult circumstances. In this way, you can take note of those whose energy is invigorating, and enjoy the stimulation of their company and, where necessary, distance yourself from those who drain you.

Second sight

'Second sight' is often used to describe the abilities of psychics and mediums, but taken literally it explains how you can first experience a visual connection with Spirit – by using your secondary awareness. I believe that when your focus is distracted elsewhere, Spirit come in through the corner of your eye. What you see through your peripheral vision is often Spirit getting your attention, not just a trick of the light.

Those in spirit don't want to frighten you and so they will only communicate with you in a way that feels natural, rather than disturbing. If you are unused to seeing Spirit, imagine how you would feel if suddenly you saw an apparition standing right in front of you! The reality could be shocking. Because I am accustomed to seeing Spirit, or my spirit guides, they will appear to me in any way they choose. I have seen people in spirit directly before me, just as if I was in the room with a friend. From the corner of my eye, I have seen images above and below a person and, in some cases, superimposed over them. On one occasion, I mistook a spirit image for the person in the room, and only realised this was the case when the appearance of my client altered before my eyes – the form of the person in spirit would look as solid as my living client, but when the spirit began talking, their form would start to fade. I asked these spirits not to manifest, not only because it confused me, but because they would use up all their energy in remembering their physical bodies. I asked: 'Look, if manifesting takes up too much of your energy, just give me a sense of your character, let me hear you and feel you.' Consequently, fewer spirits manifest during a reading.

Those that do not manifest are able to stay with me longer during a reading. I can still talk to them – I can even tell if they are pulling a face – because I can feel it, and I can describe their appearance, because I have learned to see without seeing.

So how do you start 'seeing?' It can begin with the sense that someone is standing next to you. Commonly, this can happen when you're engaged in conversation with someone else. Sometimes you may feel that someone was standing there, but had moved away just seconds before. This is Spirit making their presence known in a gentle way. It is never their intention to scare you or harm you, as this would cause you to retreat rather than become more open to communication.

When I think about Spirit around me, I believe that Spirit stands as an invisible presence on the edge of our senses. When you accept Spirit at your side, subtle visual contact often follows. And when you come around to the idea, Spirit literally comes around to you, moving from the edge of your vision to the foreground. Spirit will only communicate in a way that is comfortable for you. When you are ready, the messages will become stronger – you will see more, feel more. Whatever you see or hear, you will recognise the presence of Spirit by a sense of warmth in you, an inner knowing. You feel love inside, because love is the reason that Spirit will come to you. I have never experienced Spirit in any other way.

Although I communicate with the deceased every day, I can never assume that Spirit will contact me in a particular way. This is even true of close friends and family who have passed over – I knew them in life, but it doesn't mean that I will know how they may want to attract my attention after death.

When my father passed away several years ago, I asked the priest if I could say something about him at the funeral. Even so, I was really unsure if I could cope with standing before everyone and keep my voice steady. I really wasn't sure what to do. So, the same day, I asked my father in spirit for guidance; and he told me to make my speech.

At the funeral service, I stood with my family awaiting the priest to beckon me to the pulpit. I turned to look at the coffin, decorated with a wreath of poppies and a union jack, and there I saw my father, crystal clear, having a whale of a time. I was astonished and nearly burst out laughing – he was practically lounging on his coffin, one leg draped over the other. His customary pint of beer was set down next to him. With a whisky chaser in one hand, a cigarette in the other, and a smile all over his face, he nodded at his coffin then looked right at me. *'Nice,'* he quipped.

I didn't see my mother at her funeral. I was only twenty-seven when she died, and I was terribly upset. I didn't know if I could expect to see her or not, but she didn't appear to me. This was unusual, because I have always seen the deceased at every funeral that I have attended. The recently deceased are always joyful. At one Quaker funeral for a close friend of mine who had sadly died from cancer, I saw my friend in spirit dance down the aisle, free of pain and so happy. I believe that everyone attends their own funeral in spirit: they are always present. I now believe that I didn't see my mother, because she had already communicated with me in her own way.

In the days after my mother's death, before the funeral, I wondered if I would see or hear her in spirit. That day I was missing her terribly. The answer came the next morning, and the two mornings after that. She called the whole family – all five of us – at 7am. I've always been hopeless at getting up in the morning, and used to rely on my mother to rouse the household; she would open the door and call up the stairs every day. That morning, when I first heard her voice, she named all of us, just as she used to – me, my husband Michael, my son and two daughters. I momentarily forgot that she had died, and rushed downstairs only to find that she was not there. But then the realisation dawned that this was her way of saying that everything was all right and that things were as they should be. What was particularly unusual, though, was that all the family heard and recognised her voice. Usually, only one person senses someone in spirit, but this was communal.

So, you can't always know how Spirit will come to you. It may be the spirit of a loved one, your spirit guides or those of someone close by. You may hear, see, feel, smell or even taste their presence. The key to sensitivity is to be open to communication through every sense you possess.

> *Spirits stand at the edge of your vision; what you see out of the corner of your eye is not imagination, it is someone letting you know they are there.*

THE EXERCISES

The following exercises demonstrate the sensitivity techniques that I use in my workshops. I know that they have benefited many of my clients. The exercises are remarkably simple – and they work. Sensitivity doesn't need to be complicated. Each of you reading this book will experience the exercises in a way that is unique to you. You may find it useful to keep a diary of sensitivity over the coming weeks to help you chart your changing awareness.

When making this spiritual journey, make sure you are not going to be disturbed. Lights on (if it's evening), and no distracting music (even meditative music), as the essence of the exercises will be lost. In silence, the pictures, sounds or feelings that you may experience will then be pure.

1 Sensing energy with your hands

Healers generally work with the one of the three principal energy fields surrounding the body in three
layers: the emotional field, the auric field or the
etheric field (*see* Chapter 4, page 147).

* **The emotional field** forms the largest and outer-
most layer around the body and mirrors a person's
emotions. For example, it can be tight or expan-
sive, bright or dull, depending on how they are
feeling. It explains why we instantly connect with
some people on 'sight', but not others. You can
also make a soul connection through the emotional field – when you instantly trust someone
you've just met.

* **The aura** is the second layer beneath the emotional
field and is the reflection of the wellbeing of the
physical body. I do see people's auras, although not
consistently. The colour and quality of the aura,
which extends as far as the fingertips, usually tells
me if someone has any health problems.

* **The etheric field** is closest to the physical body.
It acts as the memory of the physical body, such
as when someone loses a limb and they still
sense its presence. The etheric is the body that a
returning spirit puts back on in order to appear to
the living.

Sensitivity is a response to the energy of all three of these fields. You can use your hands to sense a person's energy and read it. When you do this, you are aiming eventually to sense all three fields – their emotional, auric and etheric fields – and be able to interpret what you are sensing from that person.

For this exercise, you will need a partner to work with, someone you are comfortable with. You should practise the exercise facing one another.

1 Stand facing your partner, and stand well back from one another – 6–8 feet or so. Let your arms rest loosely by your sides. Open your palms outwards.
2 Now focus your awareness on your palms. Now walk very slowly forwards towards your partner. You may feel a slight tingling in your palms and fingers; it's very subtle.
3 As you walk closer towards the other person's energy fields, you may feel a change in temperature. As you make contact with the other person's energy field, you'll feel a buoyancy, as if you're pushing a bubble of air. Stop walking and move your palms back until you feel that resistance again.
4 Gently explore the edge of your partner's emotional field. In some places, you may find that you

can move your hands over it, as if you're feeling the surface of a bubble of air. Don't think about what you're sensing, just feel it. You will get a sense of what this person is feeling, though it will seem as if they are your own feelings. This is how Spirit is helping you to connect with your partner's energy.

5   As you go through the emotional field, be very aware of your hands until you come to a feeling of change – this could be a temperature change, either warmer or cooler. You could also feel a subtle tingling in your hands or possibly all over your body. You are now touching the edge of the aura. Now sweep your hands around gently, keeping the palms flat open until you feel that there is less resistance. When you feel this place of least resistance, follow through the opening in the auric field with your hand, because this will point directly to the place in that person's body where there is a physical problem of one kind or another.

6   In order to carry on through to the etheric field you need the permission of your partner, as this is the innermost layer of protection in their energy field. Consequently, as you keep moving your hand closer, you may find that there is more resistance here. Eventually, you may sense either hot or cold under your hands. Stay in that area until whatever you are feeling disappears completely. Often, if someone has had an operation, you will find the

least resistance at that point in their etheric field, which will also penetrate right through to the outer emotional field.

What did you sense?

By paying attention to your sensations, you can begin to 'read' your partner. Your response to their emotional field will tell you how they are really feeling inside, not how they say they are feeling. For example, if someone has buried anger, you may experience this in your palms as a strong 'pins and needles' sensation, or a general prickly feeling.

If you felt less resistance in some areas of their field, or if you felt a hole, this can indicate that there is something wrong with the body. This can alert you to the beginning of a health problem. If you follow the hole with your hands and your senses, you will be able to say what you feel the problem is.

This exercise is to help you to understand your own sensing – trust what comes to you. It is important that you speak out loud the feelings you are experiencing to your partner as soon as you have them. This way, your mind does not have time to alter your immediate perceptions and you are allowing your instincts to express themselves freely.

2 Sensitive hearing

Many clients tell me their hearing becomes more acute as their psychic ability expands. When I lived in a house by the sea, I even heard morse code while sitting in my garden. I didn't know it was morse code at the time – I described the bleeps I was hearing to a family friend, who explained what it was. I would often hear the signal from a boat, and then watch it sail into view an hour or so later, with a rescue boat alongside.

You may begin to hear birdsong from half a mile away, a conversation between people in a busy supermarket or on the street. You'll know it because it works like a radar – you can't hear it, then suddenly the sound comes into range. It might sound as if I'm talking about normal hearing, but when you consciously focus on your intention to hear, you will hear more. Try the exercise below to practise tuning in to distant sound.

1 Sit in a comfortable chair, and close your eyes. Feel at peace and be perfectly still.
2 What do your hear? What is the quality of the sound? How does it feel? Do your ears ring, or tingle? Far-distant sound can feel like a subtle sensation around your ears, like tiny pin pricks.

3 Listen to the sounds of silence; it can be quite noisy!

4 Write down what you have heard, or speak it out loud.

Aural information from Spirit doesn't have to come from a distance, however. I call close-up sound from Spirit 'internal sound'. This happens when Spirit tell you something without you being aware of it. Have you ever been with someone and you are convinced that they have just said something important to you, but when you tell them, they say that they haven't said a word? This can be a sign of Spirit talking to you close up. This kind of knowing resonates on the inside. Often when Spirit speak, they speak inside of you, so you sense it as if you are receiving a message. How often have you felt that you have heard something that you know is meaningful and yet you dismiss it as your imagination? We could receive so much more guidance if we could accept these promptings as real messages sent to help us.

3 Sensitive sight

This exercise helps you to believe more actively in what you see, and expand your spiritual vision. There are two ways of seeing: physically, or externally, often beginning as a small sensation at the corner of your eye, and internally, when you see a picture in your mind's eye. These are the images that you will work with during the visualisation exercises (see page 32). Because Spirit will only appear to you in a way that is comfortable for you, to begin with you may feel a presence, rather than see an image physically or internally. The more comfortable and practised you become, the more sensitive your vision.

1 Place a candle securely on a table. (I use a light-coloured candle, because it gives clarity of vision.) Sit comfortably so that you can see the candle, and light it.
2 Focus on the flame. Don't try to draw the candle-light in to you, and don't take yourself into the flame. Just be with the beauty of the light.
3 Now pay attention to what you may see at the edge of your vision, without altering your focus on the flame. Let any colour, sensation or image register. Don't think about what it could be. Just receive it.

4 Now close your eyes. This will help you to expand what you have seen with your peripheral vision. Don't expect anything. The more you can push away your thoughts, the more clearly you may see.

4 Centring

You can practise this simple visualisation as a preliminary to any of the guided visualisations throughout this book. It is particularly helpful if you are feeling stressed, or generally out of kilter. Through practice, it can help you become more sensitive to your internal vision.

1   Visualise a candle flame, and look at the golden centre.
2   When you can do this, hold both your hands as if cupping the light of the flame.
3   Feel, if you can, the warmth of the flame.
4   Move your hands apart, stretching the golden light. Keep going until you are no longer aware of your hands and you feel the light is both in and around you.

You are now centred. You can learn to do this quite quickly, at any time when you need to take a few minutes to sit still and be quiet.

5 Opening your chakras

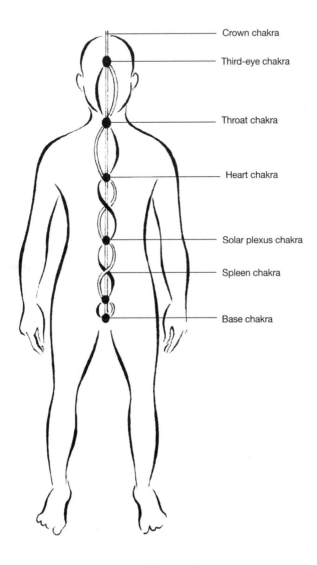

Crown chakra

Third-eye chakra

Throat chakra

Heart chakra

Solar plexus chakra

Spleen chakra

Base chakra

This is a good general exercise for daily practice in developing sensitivity, particularly when you need to feel calm and still your mind.

The chakras are the seven principal energy points on the body. They are sited at the groin (the base, or root, chakra), the spleen (or navel, chakra), the solar plexus, the heart, the throat, the brow (or third eye, between the eyebrows) and the crown of the head. There is also an eighth chakra, located above the crown, which usually corresponds to your fingertips when you extend your arm above your head (see the chakra journey exercise, page 105). In this exercise, we use the seven on the physical body. The chakras are energy centres of spiritual knowledge, through which we can access our higher selves. By opening the chakras, we open to increased sensitivity.

1   Sit comfortably, with both feet on the ground. Close your eyes, and take a deep, round breath, in and out through your nose.
2   Visualise a cocoon of white light enveloping you from head to toe for protection (see page 68). Seal it as if you were holding the air inside a balloon.
3   For the base chakra, visualise a violet flower: feel its texture, trace the outline of its petals. See the petals open, then open the centre of the flower.

Really look at the colour and detail of the petals.

4 For the spleen chakra, visualise a white daisy. Open and touch the petals, feeling its vitality. Open the centre of the daisy and look around – what can you see? Just allow yourself to experience whatever comes to you.

5 For the solar plexus chakra, visualise a sunflower. Touch it with your fingertips as its petals and centre open up to you. Its centre reveals a volcano, and deep within is liquid gold. It isn't hot; it is totally safe. You are sitting on the volcano's edge. Dive in and immerse yourself in this gold. Feel its light and energy penetrate your being.

6 For the heart chakra, visualise a delicate pink rose. Again, feel its texture. See its petals and centre open for you.

7 For the throat chakra, visualise a forget-me-not. Trace the outline of its blue petals, and watch them peel back to reveal its centre.

8 For the third-eye chakra, visualise a buttercup: open its petals and centre.

9 For the crown chakra, visualise a golden crown opening, and shining a ray of light upwards.

You are now open to Spirit in a way that you will be able to sense beings.

Now close your chakras. To do this, imagine that each chakra has two little flaps, one folding over the other. See them close, one at a time, for each of the seven chakras, and feel at total peace.

Chapter 2

Meeting Spirit Guides

My spirit guides live in my earliest memories. Their love and guidance graced my formative years, and I cannot remember a time when I did not sense their presence. To me, my guides – or 'Spirit' – were friends that not everyone else could see. My mother and Lottie, both sensitives, believed in my other-worldly confidants, but as a little girl I had not yet grasped that invisible friends were generally tolerated by other adults as a childhood game to be put away with the toys.

At that time, my spirit guides came to me day and night. I didn't think it unusual that my version of a bedtime story involved talking to five or six deceased people: together, we shared the liveliest conversations and, later, the most amazing spiritual teaching. I became used to seeing the ordinary faces of my spirit friends gathered at the foot of my bed, and me chatting about the day I'd had. I would have been three or four years old at the time, because I remember that they all followed me to school when I was four and a half. Yet my friends never frightened me, even in the dark; I instinctively knew that they were there to protect me and keep me company, especially when school days felt lonely.

The guide who was with me the most at that time was the man who I had named 'God'. I can see now that he resembled a monk, but as a little girl he was simply a man in the rough, brown suit. I talked to him as naturally as I talked to my mother and father – out loud. Clearly, 'God' was an unfortunate choice of name since I attended a Catholic girls' school in Birmingham. Within weeks of my arrival I was reprimanded by the nuns for taking the Lord's name in vain.

I recall one nun asking me who I was talking to.

'It's God,' I replied.

'Don't blaspheme!' she shouted. 'Who do you think you are?' I knew that she was really angry with me, but I was indignant. God had never told me his name, but I had just made the assumption: he was *my friend God*.

'It is God – it *is*!'

And so it went on. I wouldn't back down, so I kept being smacked by the nuns.

One day, God said to me: 'Don't worry. It only hurts for a little while. One day, you'll be able to teach them.' At this time I only understood this as the possibility of happy vengeance: I would be the nuns' teacher so I could smack them back, just like a child. Yet God was teaching me already, in his own subtle way. Every Sunday in church I remember him whispering in my ear, translating the Latin sermon and explaining its meaning in a language that a five-year-old could understand.

Just as God was my spiritual mentor, he was also my superhero. He held my hand as we crossed the road, and once he jerked me back to the safety of the pavement when I ran ahead towards oncoming traffic. There were so many little instances when I physically felt his hands around me, stopping me hurting myself. I can't remember them all, just as I cannot remember everything my mother did, day in and day out, to protect me as a child. But what I will always remember – and still feel to this day – is having my hand held throughout every step of my life.

When I communicated with my spirit friends as a child, I had no real understanding of death. I didn't really think about the previous lives that my spirit friends had lived. And I didn't think that they had experienced physical death. I simply accepted them as they were. I do remember asking some of them where they were from, and sometimes I would be shown a picture. In one instance I was shown the image of an old house. I didn't understand that this particular spirit had physically lived there – instead I assumed that as I didn't recognise it, it meant that they didn't come from Birmingham, or at least our street in Birmingham.

After my mother asked me not to talk to others about my friends, I rationalised to myself my contact with them by saying, 'Well, you're not really dead, are you?' I simply accepted my friends as they were. The idea of death didn't fascinate me, or worry me – until my uncle died.

Uncle Charlie wasn't a blood relative, but a family friend. I remember my spirit friends telling me after his wedding that he wasn't going to have any children. I tried to tell people this, but they took no notice of me. Sadly, he committed suicide. Afterwards, I remember going to his house, where he took his life, to see if he was still there. Somehow I wanted to be sure that he was comfortable. But I didn't see him, hear him or feel him. That was a strange, empty feeling. It was at this point that I realised that adults were upset by death, so I started to think that I should be worried about it, too.

Shortly after the funeral, I met Uncle Charlie again. There was a blanket of sadness in the house. I remember that it was around Christmas time, because the fire was lit, and we were all assembled around it. All my family were there, and Uncle Charlie's mother and other members of his family too. I looked over to a chair in the living room and saw him sitting there, just as he'd done when he was physically alive.

'Can I sit on your lap? I asked, and he replied that this was fine. So I went over to the chair. But I couldn't feel him at all, as if there was no lap to sit on.

'I can't feel you,' I said.

'Yes, but you can see me. You just tell them I'm all right.'

So I blurted it out. 'Uncle Charlie's all right, and he's here and I'm sitting on his lap.'

'Yes, Dorothy, keep quiet now. Take no notice of her,' my father admonished.

'But he's *here*!'

'No, Uncle Charlie's dead.'

'No, he's not. He's just not here, like us, but he's not dead.' There. I had said it.

But my father found this really hard to accept. He tried to explain to me what death was all about, as this was the first time we'd ever talked or discussed it. It must have been doubly difficult for him, too, as my mother was in hospital at the time, seriously ill with tuberculosis. He said: 'There are times when people die and you think that you can still see them.' He was talking from his experiences as a soldier during the war. 'But you can't, you know,' he continued, 'you are just imagining it.'

Then Uncle Charlie talked to me again. He gave me a message so that everyone would believe me. Charlie said: 'I knew that you never wanted me to marry my wife.' There was complete silence in the room. Dad said, 'You must have guessed that.' I think this was because earlier the family had been talking about Charlie's widow, and how she may have driven him to take his own life. But Charlie just said, 'It's okay, I got the message over.' He had just wanted me to let his mother know that he was okay.

As I got older, God didn't come so often, although he has stayed with me throughout my life. As an adult, I can understand his presence more deeply, but I often think fondly of how he appeared to me as a child. He gave me a sense of being totally loved and protected, no matter what I did.

We all have a main guide in life, who is with us from birth. We may meet him or her at any time of life – I did not meet my main guide until I was in my thirties. You will meet your main guide when he or she chooses, not when you choose. In addition to your main guide, there's a supporting cast of other guides and you may know them for many years before meeting your main guide.

Your main guide is constant, but your other spirit guides may change, just like earthly friends; we always meet new people who more closely reflect the immediate aspects of our dreams, personalities and desires when we are ready to grow. Our guides therefore change as our lives and experiences expand. But when you meet your main guide, it means that your outlook on life is about to change significantly.

When I reached my thirties, I think that Spirit decided that I was ready for the next instalment of spiritual growth. My main guide, who has shaped my thinking beyond belief, is always by my side when I am giving readings, and after he first came into my life I began to read spontaneously for friends and acquaintances. Until that time, I had never envisioned that in the future I would be reading professionally. His name is Li Ching, and I met him through a spiritualist church.

Li Ching came in the midst of a spiritual drought. Having been 'diagnosed' with ESP when I was ten years old, because of the fear in my family about sensitivity, I had decided to try to ignore my guides. I knew that they were still with me, but I didn't want them to talk to me too much. And I had enough to distract me: I had been married to my husband, Michael, for over ten years, and had three children.

This chapter of my spiritual journey came about after Michael and I decided that we wanted to run a restaurant together. That decision brought me into contact with the world of Spirit again, and I know that Spirit were guiding me towards the premises we found – a fifteenth-century cottage restaurant in Ringwood, Hampshire. It was a very interesting place psychically, with a reputation for spiritual activity, and it often attracted mediums who had heard of sightings of apparitions there. There was a royal charter in the house, dating from the reign of Charles I, and the grounds had been used as a billet for soldiers and their horses. I knew about the billet from spiritual experience rather than the local guide-book. When we arrived, I had wondered about the long row of indentations in the brick wall at the bottom of the garden. Shortly afterwards, I heard the sound of horses – their hooves, their movement and neighing. We did have a horse, but this sound wasn't coming from our stables. I followed the sound to the garden and there I saw horses in spirit, tethered to metal rings attached to the wall; soldiers were milling around them. The house was also known for its ghostly smugglers, who were seen carrying barrels through the garden up to the house.

Soon after we moved in, Michael admitted to me for the first time that he had seen people, or ghosts, in the house: one spirit gentleman he named 'Charlie' (whom we later identified as the Duke of Monmouth, whose troops were billeted in the grounds). Visitors to the restaurant talked freely about their sense of the place, and some were sensitives who openly acknowledged their beliefs and the purpose of their visit. This was a revelation: I could actually talk about Spirit with people who were alive! I reflected, too, on the extent of my past secrecy. Aside from my mother, the only other people with whom I had been able to discuss the subject were those with first-hand experience – my friends in spirit.

One evening, a customer I had been talking with persuaded me that I should visit a local spiritualist church. Initially, I rejected her suggestion. I had never heard of a spiritualist church and, given my Catholic upbringing, the idea of any church didn't sit comfortably with the Spirit I knew. But my fifteen-year-old daughter, Nicky, was encouraging and she offered to accompany me. In the end I gave in and agreed to go, derisively commenting, 'Full of old cranks, I'll bet!'

To my relief, when we arrived I saw that the church was not a church as such, but a meeting room in a Regency house. We were greeted by lovely people and they welcomed us as long-lost friends. All the same, I was merely going through the motions – sitting unobtrusively at the back of the hall, joining in with the odd hymn and prayer.

A lady then stood up to introduce the medium, who duly took her place on a dais. The assembly was quiet and reverent. I remember thinking to myself, 'OK, if she's any good I want to hear something.

I am not coming here and wasting my time.' The medium said, 'I've got someone called Grace here, and she is giving you a tulip.' Grace was my mother's name. It was what I wanted to hear – and exactly what I was scared to hear. It confirmed that others were sensitive too, and I knew that this meant things would change for me. I knew that the tulip signified that my abilities were about to blossom. My world was about to expand beyond recognition.

The medium continued. 'Grace is asking me to tell you that the brick wall she told you about is now a door. She loves you very much, and she's happy. Does that mean anything to you?' I wanted to scream out, 'Oh yes, it's my mother!', but I just said, 'Yes, thank you, OK'. My mother was speaking metaphorically here, and it was a phrase she had often used during her life-time to tell me that when things are tough, there's always a way through. I was so taken aback because, other than myself and my aunt Lottie, I had never met anyone else who could channel Spirit. Later, after the service, I talked with the medium about her work. Her name was Ruth Martin, and she invited me to her house the next Monday evening. I had no idea what it would involve, but I knew that I had to go.

When I arrived at Ruth's, four others were present. I didn't know any of them, and we had barely exchanged glances before Ruth turned out the lights and switched on a blue light. I never asked Ruth about this light, so I do not know why it was blue – I simply accepted it. So there I was, waiting in the dark with a group of strangers, feeling odd, but quite safe. I was sitting there looking at the blue light, musing: 'Well, I could always do Carl's [my son's] room in that colour', and suddenly I heard a swooshing noise to my left side – I can only describe it as the sound you hear when you put your ear to a sea shell. A man came close to me, and I could see his every detail. He was Chinese, dressed in a beautiful jacket made of purple satin, embroidered and edged with gold. He wore a little black hat, also trimmed with gold to match his jacket. He introduced himself to me as Li Ching, and told me that I may call him by that name. I said, 'OK', and he bowed his head and went away. To be honest, I didn't think too much more about it.

Some time elapsed, then Ruth spoke again. We went round the circle in turn, describing what we had seen. When it was my turn to speak, I told them about Li Ching.

I returned to Ruth's circle the following week, and Li Ching came to me again. This time, he pulled a great old-fashioned gold key from his sleeve and handed it to me. 'Now you have it, now you must use it,' he said. I thanked him, but did not think to ask him what door the key would open. He said, 'You have no need to come here again. We do not wish you to read books [he always says 'we']. We wish to teach you ourselves; we do not wish you to sit in a group. Your teaching is to be pure. Thus it will continue.' He spoke to me then just as he does now, in that same formal way. But when it came to sharing my experience with the others, I didn't reveal that Li Ching had told me that I did not need to return to the group. I didn't want them to think that I thought myself above them or anything like that. But as I was leaving, Ruth turned to me and said, 'You won't need to come any more'. At that point I realised the value of this lady. She sensed what Li Ching had said and what he had shown me, and her sensitivity was a great example to me.

I now know that the key showed to me by Li Ching was the key to great knowledge from Spirit. To me, it symbolises that there is no door that can't be opened. Of course, I didn't comprehend this at the time, but looking back I can see that Li Ching was announcing my initiation into learning. I was to be taught about Spirit *by* Spirit.

From then on, Li Ching took over and my spiritual education began. I would go along to a bookshop, pick up a book and it would fall out of my hands; after this had happened several times, I began to understand that Spirit did not want me to read whatever book I had chosen for myself. Nowadays, the opposite happens. Sometimes books fall off the shelf for me to read. Li Ching has taught me many different ways of seeing the world, which you will read about throughout this book.

Who are spirit guides?

All humans and animals have their own spirit guides. Everyone comes into this world with a main guide and a guardian angel, who stay with you for ever; your other guides, or 'supporting cast', follow, and any of these could be a member of your family who has passed over into Spirit. Our main guide is a person we spent time with in a previous life: they have lived physically on Earth, and they agree to return and protect us. In my case, I was a student of Li Ching and I know from my conversations with him that he taught me philosophy.

A client of mine, a neurosurgeon, has a guide who looks over his shoulder when he operates on people. He later discovered his spirit guide had been an eminent surgeon in his day, practising in the same hospital where this client now works. You and your spirit guides will have shared a deep interest and concern for one another in your past incarnations, although in my experience this rarely goes as far as to having been lovers. You may have loved these people as relatives, but the vital point here is that your guides acted in a capacity of guardianship in your previous lives.

Spirit guides and free will

You guides cannot interfere in your life, but they will warn you if you are about to do something that won't further your interests. This is because they know your life map. On your life map there are principal routes and junctions, but there are also detours etched along the way, which you may choose to take at any time. If a new path doesn't lead to fulfilment, you may come to a dead end and turn back to the destined route. This is the exercise of free will. You decide when and where you go, but your guides act as signposts along the way.

It is we, though, who are responsible for our blueprint, or life map. I know through my teachings from Spirit that we write the blueprint for our own lives in our 'in between' life, when we are in spirit waiting to be born into this life. The soul knows what the soul needs to learn in the next life. This is why, when we are on track in life, we feel totally in tune with ourselves and with everything around us. If we stray from our destined path, our guides help direct us back, guiding us through our feelings to help us sense the best way ahead. When we go against our guidance, doors seem to close – whatever we are trying to do just doesn't work out. If you are still, you can listen to your guides and feel what you are being guided to do. It's important to take this time out to listen: so often, it's only when things go wrong that we say, 'I *knew* I shouldn't have done that.'

Everything you have ever done – the incorrect actions you have taken and the wrong paths you have travelled – make you who you are right now, but there's no fear, and no judgement, in the spirit world. When we are born, our souls are pure and stay pure throughout life. The imperfection is in our personalities, not our being-ness. I remember Li Ching's teaching on the subject: 'Why do you stress yourself so much in trying to be perfect,' he asked, 'when there is only perfect imperfection in humans?'

Spirit come to us to teach us the value of unconditional love, for ourselves and others. Li Ching taught me that you must love yourself first before you can love someone else. I have met many people who don't like who they are, but they do have the potential for change. They can exercise free will.

> *When your guide draws close to you, you will know because you feel a welling-up of love. You will want to share this with others. When you feel these waves of love, a sense of wellbeing and deep knowing often follows.*

Spiritual identity

Your guides may tell you their names, but I have many guides who have no name. It doesn't matter whether you have a name for them or not, because they don't mind what they are called. It's only humans who want to identify. I simply call one of my guides, my American-Indian eagle friend, who appears to be half-man, half-bird. When he came to me, I felt the wings of a large bird swoop past my face. I knew that this bird was an eagle, with brown and white feathers. I then saw the face of a Native-American. He has no name – or none that I have been told directly.

Another of my guides is a vivacious Hungarian Romany lady. She appeared to me right at the end of a day, when I had been chatting with my other guides. She wears colourful clothes and jingling jewellery. Her name is Minja, and she insisted that I use a 'j', not a 'y', in the spelling. She also told me to pronounce it '*Min-ya*.'

As there is no status attached to spirit names, there is no hierarchy of spirit guides. My guide, Li Ching, looks high-ranking, but be prepared to accept anyone as your guide. He or she may look like a peasant! No matter – the wisdom is equal. They all come to us with love.

People often ask me why so many guides are Native-American, Chinese, Romany or monastic. I believe that this is because these cultures and traditions evolved spiritually a long time ago. Indigenous or native peoples have great knowledge; when they return to spirit and chose to become our guides, they are much more in tune with their spiritual identities because in life they worked at an advanced spiritual level. As more people acknowledge the presence of their spirit guides, so we can all begin to access their ancient wisdom.

Remember, the guides you meet now will be right for your stage of spiritual development. Sometimes a new guide may enter your life to teach you about a particular aspect of spirituality, such as healing. When this happens, it means that you are ready to learn.

At times, you may feel alone or unable to feel the presence of your guides. This can happen when you are going through a period of transition – a little like having one foot poised in mid-air as you climb the stairs. Initially, change can often make you feel uncertain or a little shaky about your ability to make a clear decision. What is happening is that a new guide has stepped into your energy, to help you learn the lessons appropriate to your next stage of development.

Animal spirit guides

Many people have animals as spirit guides. I have a green tiger who sometimes follows me around – if I'm feeling nervous about something, I get a glimpse of him. When you need protection, look out for animals because you may experience your spirit guide communicating through an animal to show you that you are safe. A black cat crossing your path, for example, has always been deemed lucky, but some people know that this is also a personal sign of protection from their guide. As your sensitivity heightens, you will naturally find yourself noticing more animal activity, and may even begin to communicate with animals directly (*see* Chapter 6, 'Talking with Animals').

Human guides for everyone

Some guides take human form on Earth, and act as spirit guides for everyone. They don't have to be Mother Teresa or the Dalai Lama, either. You can often recognise them by the guiding job they do: the lollipop man seeing children across the road; an ambulance driver; a sympathetic assistant at the chemist's; the receptionist at the office whom everyone confides in. You can also identify them by the quality of their presence. There is an aura of stillness and peace around them, and they engender a feeling of safety. Others naturally unfold to them and they often give words of comfort and wisdom. Think about the people in your life whom you trust, outside your immediate friends and family, because there will be a guide among them.

Acquaint yourself with your guide by acquainting yourself with the touch of your guide. Allow yourself to be sensitive, and you will expand and receive guidance.

Feel that the strength of your guide is with you.

Signs of your guide's presence in daily life

I have explained in this chapter how I sense the presence of my guides through recognising an associated sensation. This can range from sensing the presence of someone, to a tingling on your skin, a glimpse from the corner of your eye, even a murmur in your ear. This can happen at any time, not only when you are meditating to meet your guide or ask a question. You may get a particular sensation when you are driving, shopping or talking to friends. However fleeting it is, take notice of it; if you can, write it down in your diary of sensitivity (*see* page 23).

As you develop your sensitivity, pay attention to all your feelings. Don't expect too much too soon – at first, you may see only a little part of your guides at the edge of your vision, and when you look around no one is there. If your guides choose to show themselves and you have your eyes open at the time, try closing your eyes and you will continue to see them. This is a good technique to employ when you need to differentiate between what you see and what you think you see.

You may be more alert to your guide's presence when you are waiting for an answer to a specific request for help. The sensations you will experience will be non-verbal messages; let these feelings expand, so that the message becomes clearer. Eventually, an answer will come to you: it may be one word, or an image that gives you direction. If you don't feel comfortable with the answer, ask again until you are satisfied. It may help to ask your guides to show you three signs in your daily life, to make you sure of their communication.

One of my clients had three signs that his life was about to change. He was working as an aerial camera operator, and had applied for a job in Canada. He had been interviewed, but he didn't think he was qualified enough to be offered the position. During his reading, however, I was told by Spirit that he would have a future in Canada.

Shortly after the reading, the first sign came – a flyer pushed through his letterbox, with the word 'Canada' emblazoned on it. The second sign was 'Canada' in the headlines of his evening newspaper; and the third, a billboard advertisement for the same. The advertisement appeared on the regular route he drove every day, but he noticed it on that occasion for the first time.

This was several years ago. He was offered the job, and his career flourished; he is now a well-known film-maker, living in Canada. Three signs were shown to him, but the point is that he noticed them. When you truly need an answer to a question of importance, pay attention to what is around you. Spirit will show you what you need.

Spirit guides can often remind you of their presence through animals (*see* page 181). Birds in particular are spiritual messengers, and bird feathers are common symbols of spiritual presence – spirit guides or angels (angels often leave feathers). For example, one of my clients, whose father had recently passed on, saw a bird perching on her windowsill – yet there was nowhere for him to perch, as the windows had no ledge. Through Spirit, this was her father's way of telling her that everything was all right. I also take note of all winged creatures, particularly if they behave in an unusual way. If I see a butterfly and it lands on my shoulder, for example, I know that this can be a spirit message for me.

Interpreting your guides' messages

Sometimes, my guides wake me up in the middle of the night. I am aware when my guides are contacting me because I wake up immediately, often feeling a deep tingling sensation. I don't recall an unsettling dream or nightmare, and I do not feel distressed. Instead, I experience an intense feeling of knowing.

In some instances, Spirit have woken me up to give me numbers. One Friday night, Spirit woke me up three times during the night. The first time, I was given two numbers. I wrote them down on the notepad I keep next to my bed. This happened twice more, again with two numbers each time, which I duly wrote down. I remember asking Spirit to leave me alone after the second wake-up call, but they were insistent. After writing down all six numbers, I rolled over to catch up on what little sleep I could get.

The next morning, a Saturday, I was running one of my spirituality workshops. I assumed that the numbers were for the members of the workshop, so I gave them the six numbers – when Spirit give you numbers in this way, I've learned through their teaching that you must pass them on. If you do not share the numbers and instead try to use them only for your own gain, you will not succeed.

Several years later, I learned that six of the twelve attendees had used the numbers for the lottery – and hit the jackpot. They had won several weeks after I had given them my numbers. One had used his winnings to buy a house in America; the others had shared their fortunes with friends and family.

Numbers, however, do not always mean a win. A client of mine recently told me of a dream in which she had seen a woman she believed was her great-aunt. The lady was dressed as an old-fashioned schoolmistress, standing next to a large clock. She was saying, 'Six o'clock, six o'clock', and tapping her baton to emphasise the message. For years, this client could not understand its significance. She knew that it had been important for her – she had sat bolt upright in bed at the time – and the dream had never left her memory. When she told me about it, I asked her, 'How long ago do you think this dream was?' I watched her counting the years on her fingers as the realisation dawned. 'About six years,' she replied. I felt that the time on the clock related to passing years, and that she was about to enter a new phase of her life. Spirit had also told me that she wanted to move house. She then confirmed that she had been considering a move and that this would begin an important phase in her life.

Participating in your own future

Whatever the messages from your guides, or if you have received an answer to a specific question, it's vital that you take part in a positive outcome. Just because your guides have told you that you will win the lottery, be successful in your work, or meet a wonderful man or woman, this doesn't mean that you can sit back and wait. You need to play the lottery, go out and look for a job, or be socially available if you would like to meet someone special. You have to take responsibility for your own life. This is one of the lessons that Spirit have insistently taught me, and I always try to pass it on to others.

How your guides may help you

My guides are my best friends. Even when life feels really bad, I still draw great comfort from our connection. You too can ask your spirit guides for help and guidance at all times (*see* 'Asking Your Guide to Help You', page 74). Your request may feel life-changing, or you may simply need a parking space or to get to a meeting on time. If you are a Christian, you will be aware of the biblical phrase, 'Ask and ye shall receive' – whether you are religious or not, this applies equally to the way that Spirit work. You only need to ask.

It is important to understand that Spirit is not in tune with time as we understand it. Our human lives are ruled by the clock, which is man-made.

Asking for a cab within the next ten minutes won't mean much to Spirit, but you can say 'as soon as you can' or 'as soon as is possible'. From experience I have found that Spirit does, however, recognise greater time-scales that relate to anniversaries or seasons. For instance, you can say, 'could this happen before Christmas time?' or 'I would like you to help me find a new house by Easter.' Occasionally, I have set a deadline of weeks and Spirit have worked to that deadline for me. In general, though, when developing your sensitivity it is best to avoid the language of our time (unless it is essential to your request) in order to focus on how, rather than when, Spirit may answer your prayer. If you focus exclusively on the future, you may miss the signs from Spirit in your immediate daily life. Think in the 'now' as much as possible.

Be specific

Other than the time-scale, in every other way you need to be specific when making a request to your guides. If you wanted to meet a new partner, detail exactly what kind of person you would like to meet – their looks, status and passions. A client of mine wrote down exactly the kind of man she wanted in her life. He had to be intelligent, musical, reasonable looking, single with no children and spiritual. And she did meet someone who at first glance fitted the bill – until she discovered that he was an evangelical Christian! Her spirituality is less orthodox, and so she felt disappointed. I explained to her that Spirit had given her exactly what she had asked for. I advised her that the next time she asked her guides for help, she could ask for a man who is 'spiritually in tune with me'.

Another female client consulted me while in the throes of an acrimonious divorce. She didn't have much money, and I recall her saying to me, 'All I want it £100,000.' This was to enable her to buy out her ex-partner and stay in their home. To her amazement, the following Saturday she won £104,000 on the lottery, almost exactly what she had wanted. Ironically, of her own free will she had limited herself to £100,000 – otherwise, I believe that she would have won hundreds of thousands of pounds. This really goes against the grain for many of us, because ego and abundance are often confused. We are told, 'Don't get too big for your boots', but in reality asking for what you want is not about ego – it is about genuine, specific intent.

Ask from a place of abundance

A friend of mine once described her mother as 'a walking scarcity conversation' because in her mind, she never, ever, got enough – of anything. When we feel like this, it's tempting to plead for help. But although Spirit doesn't judge us on our circumstances, pleading muddies our intent. By focusing on what is missing rather than on the potential of having what we truly want we may create energetic misdirection. Our message to our guides is beset by the fear of continued impoverishment rather than the richness of possibility.

The universe is limitless in its abundance. Never plead, just ask. You don't need to be desperate. There is enough love, money, support and inspiration in the world, and the universe, for you and everyone else. Simply say, 'I would like ...' Trust and accept that Spirit will answer your call.

If you work from a place in your heart that feels insecure or defensive, energy won't flow easily. Here's how I made that discovery.

Several years ago, I was asked to give a talk about my work as a sensitive to a group in Middle America – I won't say exactly where, but it was in the 'Bible Belt' and I was worried about criticism. I knew of one person attending who appeared to be against me, so I more or less addressed my potential critic throughout. Instead of assuming that most people were interested and open-minded, I believed that everyone else was sceptical too. I limped through the talk, and when I finally stepped down I didn't feel satisfied with my performance at all.

At the following reception quite a few attendees approached me, and we started chatting. After a moment or two a small crowd had gathered, and I ended up giving the talk that I'd intended to give – before my attack of insecurity. People responded so positively, asking me questions and sharing their own experiences. Eventually, I had got to do the work I wanted, second time around. Spirit taught me then that doing the best for myself also meant doing the best for the majority.

It is the same when asking Spirit for help with love and relationships. It's not selfish to want good things, because when you get them you can share them with others. When you are happy and with people you love and who love you, the love is multiplied; other people close to you also feel it and benefit. So, whatever you ask Spirit for, be specific, feel the possibility of abundance and ask for what you want 'for the good of myself and all others'.

THE EXERCISES

All you need when using these exercises is belief. The most important thing when contacting your guides is to have trust and faith – not necessarily religious faith, but faith in a divine presence. Your guides don't need someone who is highly religious; in fact, they don't need anything from us, only that we ask them to be near. Sometimes they will come close to you without you realising it, but once you do you will feel them, sense things and may even see them.

1 The light cocoon

I use the light cocoon when contacting my guides because it protects me. Some people use a band of light for protection, but this invisible band doesn't cover your whole body. It is important to protect your whole body – not because there is any danger in the spiritual practices in this book, but so the cocoon protects you from any negativity and ensures that everything you receive is positive. I also use the light cocoon before going anywhere where there will be a lot of people, such as while travelling, because it protects me from absorbing negative energy from others.

In this book, use the light cocoon before you embark on Meeting Spirit Guides (see page 37) and all the spiritual journey exercises. There's a reminder in each exercise to do this, just in case you forget, so book-mark this page for future reference.

1 Sit comfortably, with your feet on the floor. You don't need music, just peace and quiet. Close your eyes. You can see more with your eyes closed than with your eyes open.
2 Take a deep, round breath, in through your nose and out through your nose. Be comfortable.
3 Visualise a cocoon of silk light, like watching

candy floss going round in a barrel. I see it as white light. You may see a different colour.

4   Now, the light cocoon encircles you in a clockwise direction: your feet, ankles, shins and knees, swirling upwards to your thighs, wrapping around your hips and waist, then your chest, and up and around your shoulders. It gets lighter all the time as it spins around your head, spiralling higher just above your crown.

5   Seal the cocoon by imagining that you are holding an inflated balloon, pinching the top with your fingertips to prevent any air escaping. At this point, you may also see a symbol (see below). If you don't, this is fine – just let go of any expectation and accept what comes to you. Let it happen.

What did you sense?

You may have seen a symbol when you sealed your cocoon, but don't worry if you didn't – I didn't see any for years. But after years of having no expectation, I witnessed a gold cross, spinning towards me. I see it now every time I protect myself with the light cocoon. It's not a crucifix – the arms of the cross I see are of equal length. Bright gold and shiny, it looks to me like two gold bars, and for me it represents spiritual light.

Over the last sixteen years of workshops, others have revealed to me their symbols. One was a golden acorn; another, a silver sparkling star. These symbols are not difficult to interpret. I would take the acorn to show strength from new beginnings; the star, a sign of great success. Any symbols you see will not be complicated – they are not intended to be. Spirit wants you to get the message clearly and simply.

2 Meeting your guide

This exercise is very simple. You tune in to your senses by focusing on a flower opening, to represent your sensitivity opening to Spirit. You protect yourself using the light cocoon (see page 68), and then ask your guides to make their presence felt. That is all there is to it. Don't try to hard, and don't worry if you don't sense anything. The problem will be that your thinking is obscuring your sensation. Trust and believe in the process, and accept what you experience without judgement. I know I keep on repeating this, but self-belief and acceptance are all you need.

During this exercise, you will call in your highest guide – this means that you ask the guide to come forward whose teaching is appropriate for you now. Otherwise, you might meet a guide from your earlier days whose teaching reflected your needs as a younger person, rather than the level of teaching that is right for you now.

1   Sit quietly. Still your mind.
2   Summon your light cocoon for protection. Let it wrap around your whole body (see page 68).
3   Imagine a flower – any flower you like.
4   Concentrate on really looking at your flower. Examine its texture, colour and shape. Look inside

the flower and see its energy, the life-force moving up through the stem and petals. This helps get you away from your mind-talk. This is an important technique to use when training yourself to expand the way in which you see things.

5 Call your guide to you. Ask them to step forward and give you a sense of who they are. Say, 'I call, from the highest vibration and the greatest light, my spirit guides to come close, and let their presence be known to me.'

This may sound ridiculously easy; but don't think that you can't do it. The key is not to think. Trust what you are feeling and your sense of knowing. Ask your guides to give you a feeling of their presence, so you will be able to know in your own body when they are near. Say:

'Touch me, so that I know that it is you.'

You may feel as though someone is stroking your hair, or you may get a tingling sensation on your face. Your guides may put a hand on your shoulder or legs. They will touch you wherever they can. Take notice of your body and the feelings on your skin. Receive their communication in the stillness of your little cocoon of light.

6 Thank your guides.

7   Now look again at your flower, and visualise that it
    is contained within two flaps, one inside the other.
    See its two flaps close.

If you like, write down what you have experienced.

What did you sense?

*Don't worry if you don't feel that you met your guide –
this technique takes practice. It is important to know
that your guides will always find a way to touch you
when you are ready. You don't have to see an external
or internal image of them to know that they are with
you. Did you feel relaxed and happy during the exercise? One sign of your guide's presence is a deep feeling of love, as if you're emotionally complete. You may
have felt a deep knowingness that something in your
life will come to you – perhaps that someone will give
you important information that helps you. This internal
knowing comes from your soul.*

*If you recognised your guide – human or animal –
remember that they often mirror an aspect of your own
personality. Did your contact with your guide feel natural and familiar, as if you were meeting a part of yourself? It is also very common that your guides will share
your sense of humour. How did it feel, communicating
with your guide?*

3 Asking your guide to help you

Speak or think your intent with certainty. Say, 'This is what I need, and this is what I would really like to happen [by a certain time].' Be clear and ask in the 'now'; see whatever future you would like as if it were here now. As you hold this image, you are setting your intention, and your spirit guides will hear that. They will begin to work on your behalf immediately.

When you have asked for help, let go and surrender to your guides' help.

1 Protect yourself with the cocoon of light (*see* page 68).
2 Ask Spirit to come close to you. I always say, 'In the name of God and Jesus Christ, in your name and with your will.' You can call in the name of Buddha, Allah, Great Spirit or whoever is sacred to you.
3 Call forward your spirit guides. I name those whose names I know. To the others, I say: '... and the friends who are unnamed.'
4 Next, open your chakras by visualising flowers opening at the seven chakra points of your body (*see* page 33). I usually do this because it helps me access the higher realms, but it's not essential.
5 Feel open and calm. Ask your guides to give you

a sign of their presence (*see* page 57) such as a tingling sensation.

6   Ask your guides to come closer to help you, whatever your need is. Be precise in your request, and also be careful about what you ask for. Be sure of it. Is it something you really want and need? Spirit will answer to the letter. They will be as specific in their response as you are in your request. When you ask, always add '... for the good of myself and all others.'

7   Whoever you experience during this exercise, welcome them. They do not want anything from you, only to give help and be close to you.

What did you sense?

When you call upon your guides to help you, you may also experience the presence of relatives or other loved ones who have passed over. Loved ones who are in spirit can choose to become your guides, or they may just want to be close to you. Loved ones often touch you in a way that spirit guides don't, unless they are both a relative and a guide. But don't worry about who's who – spirit guides and loved ones in spirit are your spiritual helpers. They don't need to be named.

Recognising a loved one

You are connected to a loved one in spirit by a bond of love. This bond is never broken.

You can ask loved ones to touch you, and their touch will be gentle. In my experience, you will know if you are with a relative who has passed on because they touch you in a different way to your spirit guides:

* If they touch your face it will feel like a cobweb.
* You may think you have a hair over your face and feel it being brushed away.
* Sometimes, they may blow on you – very gently. They have an ability to move the air around you.
* You may feel goosebumps on your skin, or as if your hair is standing on end.
* You feel a deep smile inside.

You can ask for their help, just as you ask your spirit guides for help.

Remember that loved ones in spirit want to help us in life. By doing so, it helps them progress. They *choose* to be around us; they are not unhappy souls, trapped in a world in between. They will move on when they choose to. It's also important to note that if anyone becomes obsessive about being in touch with those who have passed over, Spirit will not communicate –

they retreat. So there is no danger that Spirit can take over a person's life – they will simply retire in order to protect the person's best interests.

Chapter 3

Spirit Readings

On this journey into sensitivity, you may begin to discover an increased awareness and sensitivity to other people. When you sense your guides, it's very likely that you may sense the other people's guides as well, and feel that you want to tell them what you see.

I have read spontaneously in shops and cafes, indeed anywhere when I first realised that through Spirit I could sense immediate information about a person. As I began to read professionally, I learned how to interpret what I was shown or told during a session. I've never been shown anything that was irrelevant to a client, but in the early years it took me longer to get messages from Spirit across with accuracy.

Before I began giving formal readings, I found myself giving strangers information from Spirit. This still happens now – when it feels right to do so, I pass on messages from Spirit.

One of the first instances of spontaneous reading occurred when I was shopping in my local supermarket. I noticed a woman standing quite close to me. She looked devastated, and I couldn't help going to her. In fact, I pretended to collide with her just so I could ask her if she was all right. She burst into tears.

'Do you need anything?' I asked gently.

'What I need, I can't have,' she sobbed.

I knew then that she had lost a child, and that I had to keep talking with her.

'Come on, let's have a cup I tea,' I suggested.

'I can't, I've got things to do.'

'Please,' I implored, 'I could do with a cup of tea.'

She agreed, and as we sat together in a cafe, she could not stop crying. She told me that her young son had died. A car had knocked him over and as a result he had suffered severe brain damage. She had made the hardest decision of her life that day – she had instructed that his life-support machine be switched off.

'I could cope with him lying there in hospital,' she admitted, 'but I couldn't cope with the reality – that he was brain dead. Only the machine had been keeping him alive.'

As she was talking, her son came and sat beside her. 'She's not ready to talk to you yet,' I told him.

'Yes, she will be,' he replied.

'No, she won't!' I argued. 'She won't be able to talk to you.'

'Yes, she will. You tell her.' He was adamant. So at that moment, I began to let her son do the talking.

'Your little boy is telling you about the presents you bought him, while he was in this state [on life sup-port]. And he wants his big sister to know that he didn't mind that she wasn't able to talk to him then.'

She looked at me in astonishment and said, 'How do you know this?

'He's sitting next to you.'

'What is his name?' She wanted real proof that I wasn't deranged. I had never really worried too much about names, but at that moment he simply said: 'Tony.' As if to help me, he added: 'She did tell me not to go after the ball if it went into the road, and I didn't take any notice.' I later found out that those were the last words that his mother had spoken to him. 'But I am here and I am with Jesus,' he continued, 'and I am an angel, and she won't believe it.'

'He is an angel,' she sighed. Tony was tapping on her shoulder, and said to me: 'See? She just called me an angel!'

The outcome was that this lady became a friend. She later told me that if it hadn't been for me talking to her that day, she might have tried to take her own life. I hadn't seen that possibility, only the depleted energy around her, and her need for comfort.

She told many people of my impromptu reading in the cafe, and it was not long before a number of them contacted me for appointments. This confirmed what Spirit had been telling me for some time: 'You won't need to advertise. We will send the people to you.' Spirit sent me this lady, and our few minutes together that day turned both of our lives around. I know that her contact with her son through me has given her peace of mind, and has helped her to deal with some of the despair of her loss. For me, this was an affirmation from Spirit that I could help people heal themselves, and that Spirit were right – people would find me.

Feeling empathy for a stranger is Spirit's way of putting you in their path so that you may help them.

On another occasion – again, while shopping – Spirit gave me a comforting message for an elderly lady. I had decided to go to the local delicatessen to buy some cheeses for a dinner party we were giving. I wasn't thinking about Spirit too much, just working my way through my shopping list. An elderly lady was waiting in the queue, and this time it was she who first made contact with me.

'I haven't got the right glasses with me, so I can't read the labels,' she sighed.

'It's okay, I'll read them out for you,' I offered. So I listed the cheeses for her.

'Thank you, dear.' She paused for a moment. 'Why am I tingling?'

'I don't know.'

She looked at me again. 'You're making me tingle!'

'That's because Albert is with you,' I replied. These were the words that came to me at that moment. Albert was nudging me and telling me more. He said to me: 'Go on, tell her.'

'He has just given you a red rose, to tell you that he loves you, and that he hasn't left you.' The lady looked at me with tears in her eyes. 'It's his birthday today, and it's my birthday tomorrow.' She thanked me, and we parted. Our three-way conversation had felt so natural. I trusted that she needed to hear from Albert at that moment, and I hoped that his message brought her happy memories.

Early readings

My first reading for a paying client was quite different. Everything about it felt painstaking, rather than the conversational free-flow I'd expected. This client, a friend of a friend, had recently lost her father. It took me an hour and a half to pass on four pieces of information from him, simply because I didn't realise that I could ask Spirit questions on the client's behalf. I sat opposite the client, waiting quietly for a message with absolute trust that what was needed would come to me. Her father in spirit came to me via a sound at first, not an image: I could hear a bicycle bell ringing. When I told the client this, she immediately knew he was with us, because this is how he had always announced his presence in life – by sounding his bike bell when he visited her.

Then I waited. And waited. Eventually I said to Spirit, 'Is there anything else this person should know?' and then Spirit gave me more. They did this by showing me an image of a full-scale house, then shrinking it. The miniature house was rotated, so I could see that one side of it was unfinished. I again told the client, saying that I had a toy house or Wendy house that hadn't been completed, and she confirmed that her father had been building a Wendy house for her children before he died.

I asked Spirit if there was more for me to tell, and I heard her father in spirit tell me that he loved his daughter, which again I relayed.

After the reading, I didn't charge the client. Fortunately, what little I had been able to tell her must have felt right, because she recommended me to other people.

This was a valuable lesson for me, because I learned that I had to participate in a reading. I needed to create a conversation, with me as the intermediary, and that would only happen if I asked questions. I also had to become adept at interpreting what I was being shown – which, in this next case, was not easy as the client had rigid views on what constituted validation in a reading.

This lady had consulted many mediums and attended spiritualist churches because she had wanted to hear from her deceased husband. As the reading progressed, I was shown a ring that he had bought her, and he described particular situations that made his presence absolutely clear.

'But what is his name?' she asked. I have never been great on names – so often it doesn't matter. When a spirit recalls a shared experience with a loved one it can be so much more meaningful than naming them. But if a client wants me to tell them the name of a relative, I will always ask. So I asked her husband in spirit:

'What is your name?'

I was then shown an image of the Sydney Opera House in Australia. I asked the client, 'Have you ever been to Sydney, Australia? The Sydney Opera House?'

'No, we've never been there,' she replied flatly.

I asked him again, and was shown the same image. I asked her one more time, and again she dismissed it. Some spirits don't want to tell me their name, so I left it at that.

By the end of the reading, I had given this lady many instances of her relationship with her husband, but this seemed to matter less to her than to hear me say his name.

'I'm sorry that I wasn't able to get his name,' I concluded.

'Well, it was still nice to hear about my Sidney,' she sighed. This spirit obviously had a great sense of humour.

I have found my own way to work with Spirit in a reading situation. When a client first comes and sits down with me, I tune in to that person's energy and rhythm so that during the reading we are in rhythm with each other. In workshops, when I am training people, I stress that they must find their own way of working. I always begin by saying a prayer for the person in front of me: 'In the name of God and Jesus Christ, in your name and with your will, I call forth all my friends.' I ask them please help the client, asking that the experience will be positive for them. I am not a religious person, but I have great faith. I ask Spirit, 'What shall I start with?' I may at first feel that I'm a blank page, but sometimes I hear just one word as I speak it – for instance, it might be 'decision'. I then ask Spirit what the decision is about. The words just come, and I only hear them as I am speaking.

When a client comes into my reading room, they often bring with them relatives in spirit, who tell me that they have accompanied my client on their journey to see me. These relatives often talk to me, telling me what the client has been talking about on the way. When I tell the client about this, they're amazed, as it demonstrates to them how their relatives can be around them in the present. Psychic information isn't always about the distant past; it can be very recent. For example, a lady's father had just died and he said to her through me: 'It was a close call on that bend, you know, you were driving too fast.' And she responded, 'God, I actually thought that as I went around the corner.' It was her father's way of giving her proof that he was still with her. Sometimes, a relative will share a joke with me to tell the client. Their sense of humour comes across, and this brings great healing and love.

Another lady who came to me for a reading wanted to understand why her husband had committed suicide. During her first reading, he had shown me how he had taken his life, through visual images of a bottle of whisky and some pills. He explained that he couldn't see a future ahead of him, but wanted to help his bereaved wife and children come to terms with his death. Yet he would not give me his name. 'You find out,' he told me.

This client subsequently booked another reading. Just before she was due to arrive, I went to use the bathroom – and a spirit came to talk to me.

'I want to do this in private, if you don't mind,' I told him.

'Hi, my name's Pete,' he said, then left the room.

Pete? He could have been anyone's. I was just thankful that he had left me alone.

When my client arrived for her reading, I knew immediately that Pete was her husband in spirit – the man who had previously refused to give me his name. She also confirmed the physical description I had given. Pete had wanted to tell me his name at a time of his choosing – even though it was somewhat inconvenient for me! He had sensed that his wife was coming to see me that day, and knew that I would be able to tell her that he was around. This is why I often say that a reading can begin before a client arrives.

Sometimes, there's no apparent reason for a spirit to contact me, but they do. The actor Richard Beckinsale, who passed away in 1978, has appeared to me three times, simply to say 'Hello' – I recognised him from television. I was having a bath at the time, and I saw his face. I know this sounds comical, but this is how it happened:

'Hiya,' he said.

'What do you want?' I asked.

'Just to say "Hi".'

And that was all. I have heard of some mediums who contact deceased celebrities, but I believe they should be left in peace. If Elvis wants to talk to me, he will; my work is not about ego.

Speaking with those who cannot talk

I also communicate with the living, and sometimes I speak through Spirit for those who cannot talk. One client, a very distressed mother, told me about her new baby, who was just six months old at the time. He was in hospital, as during the birth the umbilical cord had constricted his neck and deprived him of oxygen. As a result, this little boy was born severely brain damaged. He came to speak to me during his mother's reading.

'Everyone is so sad, they're not happy,' he began, 'but I am.' He had been having fits, he continued: 'I call them spasms, and they can be made better.' He told me about the little blue rabbit that his mother had bought him for his birthday, so that she would know that it was him speaking.

This lady came to see me regularly – every four to six months – for years, in order to talk with her son. When she understood that he could hear her and communicate, she began to become more sensitive to him. She learned to read the meaning in his every glance, knowing he was hearing and feeling her presence.

Since his birth, she had been preparing a case against the hospital to ensure that he would have the right equipment and medical care for his needs at home. He was five or six years old when he gave me specific advice for his mother on making the claim, describing exactly what had happened during his birth. Even for me, this was an extraordinary experience – a small child communicating through a medium to help his parent in need. He told his mother, through me, the level of compensation that she would receive from the hospital. He also told her how long he would live: 'I won't make double figures,' he stated, 'but I am not frightened.' He died just before his tenth birthday.

This little boy was so happy with his quality of life. He loved his nurse at home, and he told me to tell his mother which stories he liked best. Since that reading, his mother has helped many other people caring for disabled children.

Ethics and guidance

Spirit told me that I must keep my feet very firmly on the ground – and my head in the stars, but not in the clouds. It was very important to keep my sense of reality and I need this to be able to be the bridge between people and Spirit. Humour plays a big part in this – the rapport between the clients, my guides and myself is uppermost.

My guide, Li Ching, is with me throughout all my formal readings, and he used to tell me off if I didn't understand his teaching, particularly when I started out. In those early years he would wag his finger at me, saying: 'No. That is not correct. What we are saying is … ; repeat word for word, please.' And I would have to listen and tell the client. 'Sorry, that's not right, that's me talking.' Only then would he continue. But if I said, 'Sorry, I think I'm not picking this up quite right', Li Chung would turn his back to the wall. So in this way, he really taught me to discern between my thoughts and the words from Spirit. I will always tell my clients if I have been told off by Li Ching or another of my guides, explain that I was totally wrong and start again. I don't feel too proud to say that I have got something wrong. It is me, not Spirit, making the error. Spirit don't get things wrong; the problem is poor human interpretation. It is our responsibility to convey their meaning as accurately as we can.

My work has become no easier over time, because to me it carries a grave responsibility to work ethically. I work at it as hard now as I did when I first started out and this is no more the case than when I have given a traumatic reading. When Spirit speak, it's about universal truths but directed at the individual. I have to be able to work with my clients in a truthful and responsible way. When people come to me, I know that Spirit will say what's appropriate for them. They won't be told anything that they can't cope with.

Sometimes I see tragic circumstances for a client, but I also see that there is a point at which they may change their future. I always ask Spirit, 'What can we do to help this person to change their situation?'

One lady visited me for a reading. She didn't have a specific problem, or person that she wanted me to contact, but I immediately understood why Spirit had sent her to me. During the reading, I saw her son on a blue motorbike. His head, inside his motorbike helmet, rolled across the road. His eyes stared back at me. It was horrific.

Spirit told me to tell my client what I had seen, in order to try to save her son's life. So I explained exactly was I was seeing. After the reading, later that evening, she called me in a panic.

'My son has just put a deposit down on a new motorbike!' She was in shock, and her fear was compounded by the fact that her son had also told her that the bike he wanted was blue. She impressed upon her son just how important it was that he didn't buy it. However, he was so looking forward to riding it that his mother's words alone were not enough to dissuade him.

However, he was persuaded to come for a reading, and I read for him the next day, as an emergency appointment. Through Spirit, I saw exactly the same chain of events leading to his death in a motorbike accident. This frightened him enough to give up the bike. When he called the garage, they wouldn't refund his deposit, so he paid for the bike and immediately sold it on to a friend.

Two months later, the friend died in an accident on the bike.

I had not seen the death of this young man's friend, although it was his time to go. The son had to be helped to come to terms with his guilt, but he was not to blame. I remember feeling very sad for the other boy's family. Had I seen his demise, I would have been able to pass on any helpful information – should there have been any possible chance of saving him.

There are times when people can be stopped and saved, and other occasions when this is not possible. It is vital to be truthful to clients, but with truth comes responsibility. One young woman came to me for a reading, and I immediately knew that she would not have long to live. I asked Spirit, 'Can she be saved?' and they replied that she could not. I asked Spirit what I should say. They told me, 'Ask her what she really wants to do.'

'I would love to travel round the world, maybe go to Australia with my boyfriend,' she admitted. She had been saving up for the trip, but didn't have enough money yet to go.

'Borrow the money from your dad, and go next week,' I said.

'That would be wonderful,' she beamed. I asked Spirit to help her. She got the extra money from her father and, with her boyfriend, went travelling for

three or four months. She died of a brain haemor-
rhage shortly after her return.

The truth was that she was going to die; but she also
needed to enjoy living the remainder of her time on
Earth. Telling her of her own death would only have
caused deep distress, and possibly ruined her
chances of being happy before her passing.

I often work with, and refer other people to health-
care professionals, and some of them have asked me
about the ethics of working as a sensitive or psychic.
I tell them that, as a psychic, you must be conscious
of your motives. At times in my life I have made
poor judgements for myself when I haven't listened
to Spirit, but I never make decisions for other
people, nor do I knowingly give information that
would hurt or upset anyone. In a reading, I always
endeavour to give only positive and constructive
guidance, and to give hope, but not false hope. But I
do know that some psychics tell people things that
disturb them deeply – they then have to come to
someone like me to pick up the pieces. To give
people information that distresses them is unethical
– the priority, first and foremost, is to help people,
not to earn a living. If I were to say to Spirit, 'I need
to earn £100 today', or assume that because I have a
certain number of clients booked I will earn that

amount, it just won't happen. An appointment may be cancelled, or I might see more people than usual that I don't charge. I just trust that I will earn enough, and I always do. If we put money before the work, the work won't follow. The work must come first.

I read for many professional people, some of whom seek advice from Spirit on the financial aspects of their business. They will always be told what they need to know. One client, a successful entrepreneur, consulted me about a bid he wanted to make to buy a business – he felt that he would have to act quickly on this.

I asked Spirit, who told me that he must wait until the following Monday – and not before 9am – five working days from the date of the reading. My client couldn't quite believe this, as he was sure that this would give his competitors time to hear about the deal and outbid him. I asked Spirit again, who confirmed that he must not make an offer before 9am on the following Monday. They also told me the price that would be paid was around two and a half million pounds.

'That can't be right,' he protested. 'It's worth twice that figure, which is what I would be offering.'

Several days later, we spoke again over the telephone.

'Look, I could really lose that business if I don't make an offer now,' he told me. 'Are you absolutely sure?'

I checked with Spirit once more, and received the same response, which I relayed. By this time I was worried. Spirit had been clear, but this client was a friend, too, What if I'd got it wrong?

He decided to go with what Spirit was telling him. I talked with him over the weekend and he admitted that he was beset with worry – if he acquired this company, he knew it would be the making of his business. If he lost it, it may be years before a similar opportunity arose.

Early on Monday morning, he drove to the company's premises. He waited in his car, his eye on the dashboard clock. Just before 9am, another car pulled up and a businessman got out, briefcase and files in hand. Terrified that this man was bidding from a rival firm, the client got out of his car and approached the stranger.

'What are you doing here?' he enquired.

'I'm the liquidator,' he replied.

In due course, they agreed that the business would be sold to my client for two and a half million pounds, half of its original value.

Clients often ask me if my spirit friends advise me in my own life, and of course they do, but I cannot predict my own future. I can never predict outcomes for myself, but I know that Spirit will support me when I really need something. Years ago, I remember that I sat up most of the night, asking Spirit if I was allowed to ask for things for myself.

'This you can do,' they replied. And they added: 'We will supply a need, but not a greed.'

Telling the truth

Telling the truth to others comes with responsibility. Telling the truth is also concerned with speaking from the heart, rather than the head. You may have heard people stridently proclaiming, 'I always tell the truth. I tell it like it is.' This stance is sometimes an excuse for being tactless – as if the truth is all that matters. How you tell the truth is vitally important, as we need to be sensitive to other people's feelings.

Telling them the truth could do them no good at all if they are left feeling confused and hurt. Your intention toward that person is very important. I often liken this to buying someone a present because you have to, rather than because you want to. As far as Spirit are concerned, this is a waste of a gift. When you spontaneously buy a friend a present to cheer them up because you want to, Spirit hear you because your actions speak from the heart, not the head. The gift is appreciated, and heartfelt.

An angry mother often speaks from the head rather than her heart, because she is frustrated with her child. With my own children, I tried to speak to them from the heart as much as possible, explaining to them the consequences of their actions. It doesn't matter how young the children are, because when you speak from the heart they will always understand your intentions. But if you speak, or shout, from your head, children switch off. I always try to explain the head–heart difference to my clients and workshop students, because the definition of each is not really what you would expect. We associate calm logic with the head and emotional outbursts from the heart, when in fact it's the other way around. Talking from the heart tends to be thoughtful. It has its own logic, which is tempered by sensitivity, whereas speaking from the head often results in anger or frustration.

In fact, the head and the heart can speak the same truth; it is just expressed differently – it's not what you say, but how you say it. If I feel angry or wound up, I take a few deep breaths and connect with my heart centre to find stillness (see the chakra exercise, page 35). Then I can speak the same truth, but with more kindness. It doesn't mean that I go through life trying to please others the whole time, but I do try to speak from the heart. It is not always easy, because at times my mind jumps in ahead of me, but I know that speaking from the heart brings me a sense of deep relaxation.

Empathy

I have read for teenagers, middle-aged executives, the recently bereaved, nuns and priests, funeral directors, doctors and surgeons, celebrities, solicitors, loving parents and those who have chosen to live by violence. They all have spirit guides who they bring with them to their reading, no matter what they have done in their lives. Spirit does not judge.

It is not essential to feel empathy in order to read for someone. Empathy is sometimes Spirit's way of connecting you with someone you may be able to help, but that is all. More commonly, we get too emotionally involved with a client. Sometimes, after a particularly traumatic reading, I feel as if my heart has been wrenched because I empathise so much. It is physically painful because my heart goes out to that person. Spirit told me to keep people at a distance, but I told them that I didn't know how to do that. 'We will teach you how,' they said. Then I get on with the work and forget that I am supposed to keep people at arm's length. Suddenly I realise that I have got these hands out in front of me – not mine; nothing is said, but it is just a reminder to keep within my boundaries.

I also need to be careful in case my empathy for a client blocks my ability to read for them. Because I have also experienced difficulties in life, it is perhaps easy for me to empathise with others. However, if I were to start to speak to a client from my own experience, my mind would go blank. If I bring myself into a client's reading, Spirit have taught me that I must tell the client that it is me – 'Dorothy, speaking now'. I occasionally do this at the end of a reading, if I feel that I have something helpful to add. But I never judge, or try to make decisions for others.

Whenever you talk to someone who is distressed or badly in need of advice, take a moment to centre yourself. Send out a silent prayer, asking that you receive the words they need to hear.

THE EXERCISE

Two of the most vital questions my new clients ask me are 'How can I know the difference between Spirit and my own thoughts?' and 'How do I know if I'm making it up?'

You may be relieved to know that it is possible to learn to differentiate. Through this guided visualisation through the seven principal chakras (see page 33), you will practise putting your mind aside in order that you may sense Spirit. When you experience the sensation of spiritual contact, you will hold it in your memory and recognise it when it comes again. There are several techniques you can use and sensations to take note of which will show you if you're using your thoughts or your sensitivity. The aim of the journey is to allow yourself to be, rather than think. When you attain this state, you can be totally open to Spirit.

When you lose the thread of an image or a sensation, it is usually due to your mind getting in the way. When I practise this exercise in sensitivity workshops, I sense and see others' intrusive thoughts as shards of glass. One way to regain the open feeling you have when your visualisation is vivid is to sink into the weight of your body and sense the softness and light of your protective cocoon. Go back to your sensations and relax, rather than trying harder. This is not an exercise in concentration. Sense your senses, first and foremost.

Go with your first impressions, as your mind is unlikely to have had an opportunity to interfere with them. For example, at the first chakra you may see a violet, or you may see a different flower (the flowers I have associated with each chakra on the journey are those that I personally see). Try not to transform your first impression into something 'acceptable'; you will know you are doing this if you lose sight of your flower image – or if it just feels like hard work. It doesn't matter what type or colour of flower you see. Trust your senses, and the images and sensations they may present you with. When you can do this, you will feel free to explore your visualised landscape and connect more closely with Spirit. You will discover your own spiritual truths.

Finding your spiritual truths: a chakra journey

This journey takes about one hour – although it may feel like only a few minutes. You may find it helpful to record the visualisation, then relax and play back your tape later.

To begin, sit in a comfortable chair. Your feet or legs may become cold during the journey, so make sure that you are warm enough. Have a glass of water to hand, ready to sip when you finish the exercise. Have both feet firmly on the floor.

Now close your eyes and take a deep, round breath, in through your nose and out through your nose. Visualise your cocoon of protective light (see page 68).

You can visualise the flowers that you will be shown from a bird's eye view, as if you are looking down on a bud. For the purposes of visualisation, all the flowers have four petals. You may or may not see their other petals as you work with their images.

1 The base chakra: security and wellbeing

1 Relax, and prepare to go deeper into your senses.

2 Visualise a violet. See the first petal open. Trace around it with your finger.

3 Open the second petal, slowly. Now look deeply at the colour and be aware of how you are feeling.

4 Open the third petal, and touch it. Feel its texture. Does it feel like paper, or silk? At this stage, be careful of your thoughts intruding. Don't think about it, just feel it. Keep touching the petal and let it absorb you. Now open the fourth petal, little by little. How does this flower make you feel – thoughtful, happy, sad?

5 See the centre of the flower. Open it wider and wider, until you are looking down into a meadow. It is beautiful. Float down into the meadow and lay in the long grass. Touch the tree there, see the stream and listen intently to the sounds of nature. It's not really quiet there, is it? Stay here as long as you need to.

6 Now find a silver cord, and attach it to whatever part of your body you choose.

2 The spleen chakra: the emotional cleansing centre

1 Visualise a white daisy. Open the first petal very gently. Look at its shape – it's very different to that of the violet. Feel its delicacy.

2 Open the second petal. You can trace its outline with your fingertips, and stroke the petals.

3 See the third petal open, and touch its little veins. Be aware of the rhythm of the energy of this plant.

4 Open the fourth petal. What sort of energy does this flower have? Can you feel its emotions? How does it make you feel? Let this register. Allow yourself to expand into these emotions.

5 Look at the centre of the daisy. Watch the centre opening wider and wider, until the flower has gone. You're looking down into an opening and a pool of clear, warm water. I want you to dive in. It's perfectly safe. Be inquisitive and explore the other life forms that may be there. Enjoy yourself!

6 Collect your silver cord.

3 The solar plexus chakra: the centre of your power and energy

1 Here, we have a huge, yellow sunflower. Its centre is brown velvet. The first petal is opening. Look at its size and shape; feel and touch it. Don't let your thoughts come in. Just be aware of how you feel.

2 Open the second petal. Can you feel the strength of this petal, this flower? Feel its simplicity and magnificence. Stroke it. What does it feel like?

3 Open the third petal. Feel for the veins on the back of the petal – there are many of them. Feel them as you stroke the petal. Touch the colour, and sense if you can feel the rhythm of its energy. Feel that you are at one with it.

4 Gently open the fourth petal. What does the colour make you feel? Can you see its other petals, too?

5 The sunflower's centre is a big, round velvet cushion. You can sit on it if you want to. Feel it. When you are ready, stand back and watch this wonderful centre opening wide – and wider, until you can no longer see the flower. You are standing on the edge of a volcanic crater.

6 As you look down into this vast energy centre, you can see liquid gold there. Dive in. Be fearless. You can fly around if you want to. Coat yourself in gold, for this is power, your power. If you look around, you may see someone there on a ledge.

Don't make them appear, though. He or she may be a mentor or guide. Go to them: ask a question or two if you like.

7 Now look up and see an opening and a shower of golden stardust raining down. Stand under it. Fill yourself up with the stardust, from your feet up to your legs and torso, and from your fingertips up to your arms, shoulders, neck and head. You are overflowing and expanding as the stardust melts into your coat of gold.

8 Whenever you have low energy, you can recall the shower of stardust to replenish yourself emotionally.

9 Once again, collect your silver cord and attach it to yourself.

4 The heart chakra: the gifts of love and healing

1 Visualise a pink wild rose. Start with the first petal, opening it out. This is a very different shape to that of the sunflower. Just trace around its delicate edges with your fingertips.

2 Now open out the second petal, very slowly. Feel its surface between your fingers. How does this feel? Is it silky? Whilst you are touching it, be aware of how touching it makes you feel.

3 See the third petal open. Touch the colour. What does this colour make you feel? Can you smell it? Is this a strong petal, or is it delicate? What does this feel like? Be aware of how you're feeling, not thinking.

4 Open the fourth petal. Look at this beautiful, simple flower. It's so perfect. Is it smiling at you? How does it make you feel?

5 Now look at its centre, and open the centre out – wider and wider. And now you're looking into an exquisite cave. Step inside; it's like walking inside a crystal. Go deep, deep inside. It's very bright here. It sparkles, and makes its own light. Touch it – what does it really feel like? Cold or warm? Sharp or smooth?

6 Now journey further inside, until you come to a place where there are three doors. One by one,

open each door. Behind each door is a gift for you. Take the gift. It may not be what you think it would be, but the truth of it will reveal itself to you. These are gifts of love, and this is a place of healing. Draw in this healing every time you take a breath. Sit in your crystal sanctuary, with your gifts. Take your time.

7 Once again, take up the silver cord; make sure that it's attached to you.

5 The throat chakra: for purity and truth

1   Here is a forget-me-knot. It is vivid blue. Open the first petal, gently. Look at this colour. Feel it.

2   The second petal is opening. Touch it with your fingers, feel it with your heart. What does it feel like? Is it smooth or rough? Is it cool or warm?

3   Open the third petal. Feel its pulse, its energy. It will transfer to you its exact feelings. What does it feel like to dance with its rhythm? Open yourself up to endless possibilities.

4   Open the fourth petal. Now look at this beautiful little flower in all its glory. How does it make you feel? It is reflecting its colour and feelings to you. Feel the emotion of this flower. Be aware of how you are feeling, too. Mind that your thoughts don't get in the way.

5   Now look at the centre of this flower – the seat of its energy. Open the centre out so it expands, getting wider and wider until you are at the top of a huge, blue silk slide. You can't see where it will take you yet. Get on it, slide down and find out. You're going deeper and deeper, and now you can see a beautiful turquoise lagoon, fed by a waterfall from a warm pool. This is a place of great energy and cleansing. Go there and dive in, under the water. Have fun.

6   Whilst you're here, investigate one of the bubbles from the waterfall. Look at your own reflection in

the bubble, and hold it in your hands. See yourself with your heart, not your thoughts; see your true self, without judgement. Take your time.

7 Collect up your silver cord, and be sure that it's attached to you.

6 The brow chakra: clarity on life

1 Here, we have a yellow buttercup. Open the first petal, gradually. Now look at its shape; it's almost heart-like. Feel its texture. Touch it. Stroke it.

2 Open the second petal. Touch this colour. Does the colour rub off? Can you see a reflection in it?

3 See the third petal open. Touch it, feel its little veins and its strength. How is it making you feel? Can you feel it?

4 Let the fourth petal open. Feel the shininess of it. What is its texture? Can you truly see the gold of it? If you came closer to it, would you become gold, too?

5 Now look at the buttercup's centre. It opens wider and wider, until the flower has gone and you are presented with a beautiful marble staircase. The stairs wind downwards. With each step you take, you go deeper into the depths of your own chakra. Light is shining on you from above. Look around as you go.

6 At the bottom of the stairs is a large door. It has letters over the top of it, which spell out the word 'truth'. Now go through this door, and find yourself in a room.

7 There are three mirrors before you. Look in each one in turn, starting with the one on the left. Clean it if you need to with whatever you have to hand.

    Look in, and don't judge what you see. Look deeply.

8 These three mirrors represent the past, the present and the future.

9 Check that you still have your silver cord attached to you.

7 & 8 The crown chakra and beyond: the higher realms

In this part of the journey, we go through the seventh chakra at the crown of your head and up to the eighth chakra, which is an arm-span above your head, on the edge of your auric field. The seventh chakra is the doorway to the eighth chakra. One way that Spirit may communicate with us is through the seventh and eighth chakras.

1 Visualise a golden crown opening and light shining upward in a ray. Breathe deeply, breathing up towards a column of white light.

2 Now you are in the light, at the eighth chakra. Have a good look around. Here you can ask questions and receive answers. Be specific in your questions, then you will receive an answer. The answers will feel like a knowing, just as you knew when opening your flowers.

3 Move around and see who is there. You may meet guides and other friends or relatives in spirit. Don't have any expectation – just let them come to you. Feel the peace and love that is here. This is your place of communication.

4 To finish the journey, close your chakras. To do this, imagine that each chakra has two flaps, one contained inside the other. Close the two flaps for each chakra, up to the seventh, in turn: the base,

the spleen, the solar plexus, the heart, the throat, the brow, the crown. You don't need to close the eighth chakra, because this always stays open. Spirit are waiting for us to use it.

5 Give yourself time to relax. Stretch out your arms and legs, and sip some water. If you like, write down what you have experienced in your diary of sensitivity (see page 23).

What did you sense?

You may have been aware of some external noise during this exercise, such as the tiny hum of traffic or birdsong. This is normal, as many developing sensitives find that their hearing becomes more acute when they attune to Spirit.

Just as you may interpret any symbols you see when you seal your light cocoon (see page 68), so too can you interpret the gifts and mirror images of the third and sixth chakras. The most obvious meaning is the simplest meaning – this is not a spiritual test! Spirit uses images that are known to us as a way of communicating with clarity. The gifts are your spiritual truths.

The gifts of the heart chakra

At the third chakra, you were invited to receive three gifts. One member of a workshop admitted to me that the gifts she had seen were a chameleon, a bunch of bananas and an amethyst ring. (Remember, your gifts can be anything!) I helped her interpret these as follows: her first gift, the chameleon, symbolised her ability to adapt to circumstances, or to fit in unseen; the bananas represented abundance – in that she would be given everything she needed for sustenance; and the amethyst ring showed a spiritual bond – the amethyst is the stone of healing, and the ring symbolised the relationship. Another client received an egg, a sign of new life and beginnings.

After the chakra journey, your gifts always remain with you for life – they are never taken away. If you repeat the journey in the future, you will receive more gifts, which again reflect your needs at that time.

The mirrors of the brow chakra

After entering the sixth chakra, you were guided to see three mirrors. If the mirrors looked cloudy, your thoughts were in the way. Did you rub the mirror in order to see? If you found it hard to see into the mirror on your right (representing the future), next time stand back from it and see it as brand new, without trying to glimpse a reflection. Now step before the mirror again, and see what appears before you.

As with the three gifts, you can interpret your mirror images. One of my clients saw the following: in the mirror of the past (to her left), a soldier boy in a red and gold uniform; in the mirror of the present (the central mirror), a lady offering her a glittering silver star. She found it very hard to see anything in the future mirror (to her right) and had to look at it several times. Her first glimpse was of a smiling woman with white laundry, but this image disappeared and in its place she saw what she thought was a red stained-glass window. When she looked more closely, she realised that she was sensing a pattern of rose petals with light streaming through them. I suggested to her that the soldier boy in the left-hand mirror was one of her past lives. The lady in the mirror of the present, offering her a star, was a sign of the success and accomplishment that she would enjoy now and in the near future. The laundry woman, however, baffled my client at first. I interpreted this as a job well done – she worked hard for a living, but her laundry was white and pure. The rose petals to me symbolise love, so together her two mirror images for the future spelled out hard work, but with satisfaction and love to come.

A week or so after her chakra journey, my client called me to say that she had been offered two new work contracts.

Chapter 4

Soul Healing

Before I begin a reading, I always ask Spirit that the experience is positive for the client. As I learned more about my work through the teachings of my spirit guides, I also realised that I could give healing, if that was what was needed. I feel that healing comes by word, deed and intention. Art is also healing, as is music, dance and acting, because we enjoy them with the right side of the brain, the site of our senses. Anything that brings a smile has a healing benefit.

I see healing as an integral part of my work as a sensitive. It comes with the territory, because in a reading I give whatever is needed at the time. I will also recommend healers to my clients, if they need ongoing treatment for a physical ailment.

The healing work that I do may come in the form of emotional healing through contact with loved ones in spirit, or healing negative behavioural patterns through showing a client their cause in a past life. If it is necessary to inform a client about a physical problem with their health, I will be shown the ailment in their body, or I will sense it through the quality of their aura. So my work with Spirit encompasses healing on many levels – spiritual, emotional and physical – which is why I think of what I do as healing the heart and soul. When people's deepest needs are acknowledged, they can often begin to move on in life.

One of my earlier clients came to me as a result of an advertisement that I had placed in a local free newspaper, to run for one month. I was new to the area and, although Spirit had told me not to advertise for clients, I went ahead. The gentleman I'm about to introduce was the only respondent.

This man, in his early seventies, hadn't come for physical healing. I remember that he used two walking sticks, and wore braces and straps on both wrists; but his reason for seeing me was because he had lost his daughter to cancer. She had died very young, and he couldn't talk to his wife about it because it was too painful for her to discuss. He had been an officer in the army, spending his life in an environment in which feelings were controlled, not expressed. Now he was desperate to talk to someone about his daughter. He had not been able to say goodbye to her when she died, as she had lived far away. When the end was near, he and his wife had driven to see her, but on their arrival they discovered she had already passed away.

His reading began, and his daughter in spirit came through. She told him it was OK that he didn't get to her before her passing; that she wanted him to remember her as she used to be, before the illness.

'She's so happy,' I told her father, 'she's so pleased that she feels no more pain.' He was crying as I spoke, and he asked me if I was wearing perfume. I replied that I wasn't – I never wear perfume during a reading.

'I can smell spring flowers, freesias,' he said. 'It's her scent.'

I was then shown this man's spine. An area of it was red and inflamed. I asked Spirit, 'How can this be helped?' I had barely finished the request when I saw the healing begin. My eyes were closed, and I was then watching a Monty Python-style animation. The top of the client's head was hinged open – I even heard it creak. I was amazed at what I was witnessing. White tubes flowed out from the top of his head, and soft blue tubes of light replaced them. The blue tubes travelled down his spine, surrounding it. It felt as if the tubes were supporting the muscles around the spinal column. This may have taken minutes, or maybe half an hour had passed – I have no sense of time when I'm reading. It was the first time that I realised I could observe the healing process in action.

When the reading was over, I told him what I had seen. This gentleman accepted it and told me that he had been suffering from terrible arthritic pain. He explained that many years earlier he had trained in healing work with the renowned British spiritual healer, Harry Edwards, who had healed him of tuberculosis. This gentleman had come to me some years after Edwards' death in 1976. When he stood up to leave, I noticed that he was using only one stick.

He returned to see me a month later, and we repeated the same healing, replacing white light with blue. He continued to visit me for over ten years; sometimes he suffered pain in other areas of his body, and the healing I observed differed according to the site and nature of his pain. In those sessions he talked frequently with his daughter, and began to let go of some of the anger he felt with his wife for not wanting to talk to him about their child. He didn't use walking sticks again.

I believe that unresolved emotional pain is often manifested as physical pain in the body. What we won't, or can't, say or hear becomes trapped. This doesn't mean that every illness or condition is caused by our feelings. The gentleman I read for so many years may still have developed arthritis if his daughter had not died and he had not had to lock away his grief. But his arthritis was the only way in which his pain could show, and this exacerbated the condition. On a spiritual level, the acute arthritis was about his inability to move forwards after his bereavement. When healing takes place, Spirit may heal us spiritually, emotionally and physically. This is healing at a soul level.

The only control we have over the healing process is our intention to help.

While staying in America, I was asked to help a young girl suffering from drug dependency. Her adoptive mother hoped that maybe I could help her to save her daughter's life.

I have read for quite a few families whose children have suffered from drug addiction, and they come from every social class. In this instance, the mother was a doctor. Her daughter was sixteen years old, hanging out with the wrong people, and seriously into substance abuse, which included taking heroin. She came to me for a reading at her mother's insistence.

On the surface, she looked fit and healthy, and very well dressed. Her mother had tried to give her everything. Spirit showed her from the inside, and she looked withered. When I see drug users, their entire bodies are dry inside. (With people who abuse alcohol, I see the same effect, but only on one side of the body; I can also smell alcohol around alcoholics who are technically 'dry'.)

The girl showed some hostility as the reading began.

'You don't have to believe what I tell you, you know,' I said, 'but please, just hear me out.'

'It's no good you trying to judge me,' she retorted.

'I'm not about to do that. Please, just listen for a few minutes.'

Spirit presented her deceased grandmother and mother. She had been adopted because both women had died soon after her birth. As her birth mother spoke through me, this girl was shifting in her chair and sniffing. Her mother told her that she, too, had taken drugs during her lifetime; whilst this wasn't the reason for her death, it was a profound revelation to her daughter, making her understand that perhaps she was repeating a pattern of addictive behaviour that wasn't hers alone.

Her birth mother chastised her about her bad relationship with her adoptive mother.

'She *is* your mother,' she began. 'I gave birth to you, and died soon after. All I could do for you was to give you life. Stop throwing that in your mother's face. She's the one who has brought you up, and she loves you.

'I love you, and would have loved you had I lived. But that didn't happen, so don't blame her for it. You cannot come over here. You have tried to take your life before, but you will always be stopped.'

Then, the girl's mother in spirit showed her the possibilities of her future, with and without drugs. She was told that she would need to change her friends and get off drugs, or she would die in about five years' time.

If she chose to live, she could have an acting career ahead of her.

'Is there anything more that you would like to know?' I queried. She asked if it was really possible that she might get into acting. I told her that she could be very successful. Her whole demeanour was changing – from being defensive and angry, she softened. She realised that she had been denying her grief about being deprived of her birth mother, and punishing her adoptive mother with her anger. She talked about her drug habit, and admitted that she wanted to break her addiction.

'I wonder if I could do that,' she asked herself.

'Well, you're a very strong person; you can do it if you really want to.'

'I'm going to do it,' she stated. 'I am going to do it.'

A few months after the readings, the girl's adoptive mother told me how delighted she was with her child. She had gone into rehab, and was no longer drug-dependent. She had won a place at theatre school and, to her mother's relief, enjoyed a much better relationship with her. As she told me in a recent conversation, 'I've got my family back.'

Spirit helped this young woman to see her true path in life by healing the scars of the past. The decision to embrace her future was hers alone.

Denying the past or feeling angry about it so often stops people moving on in their lives. One woman who came to me for a reading was very depressed. She was recently bereaved, and her husband had left her because he couldn't deal with her grief.

When she came, she was accompanied by two little boys in spirit. I told her that there were two children with her, but she denied this.

'No,' she replied, 'I have only the one.'

'But there are two here.' I could see them both so clearly. So I thought that the second child must have been playing games with me. 'You are naughty, messing me about like this,' I told him.

'No!' he protested, 'She is my mummy.'

'But she's saying that you are not her little boy.'

'I am. I *am*.'

'Well, she can't accept you at the moment,' I replied. 'Maybe she's hurting too much.'

'She is,' he said, 'and I love her.'

Six months later, the same lady returned for a reading. She was in a terrible state of guilt, because she had denied the presence of her second child in spirit.

'I find it so hard to say that I have lost not just one child, but two,' she admitted. One had drowned in a shallow pond in her garden – she had found him laying face down in the water. Three years later, her second boy had had an accident while playing in a willow tree in the same garden. He had been with his friends but they had gone home, without his mother realising, so he had continued playing in the tree by himself. While climbing in the branches he had become entangled in the rope ladder, which had strangled him. She told me how she had called him in for his tea three times; when he didn't answer, she had had a sinking, nauseous feeling. Horrifically, she had found him hanging from the willow tree.

I told this lady that her children were very happy in the spirit world. I asked them what they were involved in over there, and they said that they help the spirits of children cross over, so that they would understand what had happened to them and wouldn't be frightened. They also told me how they aid and comfort the bereaved parents of those children.

At the time of this second reading, this lady had reached a turning point in her life. She had been able to acknowledge the death of her second child to someone. She came to see me many times over a period of years, and managed gradually to release her grief. She subsequently trained as a healer and, when her training was complete, the process of grieving came to an end. Of course, she will always feel deep sadness about the deaths of her two boys, but now she communicates with them in spirit all the time. They guide her, and give her the strength to give healing to others. By accepting rather than denying her terrible loss, this woman was able to live again. Her story is a great inspiration to many people who have suffered as she did. Of course, time is a great healer, although this is not what a bereaved person wants to hear. I believe that help from Spirit is an even greater healer.

Children often return in spirit to help heal their bereaved parents. One happy young girl came through to me during her mother's reading. She had suffered severe learning difficulties during her lifetime, and had committed suicide when she was a teenager.

Everyone in the seaside village she lived in had known her. At first no one thought her behaviour terribly out of character, given her eccentricities, when she waded into the sea wearing a heavy winter coat. Yet when she walked deeper into the sea, following the outgoing tide, a local man became worried and swam out to save her. By the time he reached her body, she had already drowned.

In the reading she told me that she had chosen to pass over, and was more concerned about her mother's distress regarding her funeral arrangements. Her mother had wanted her to be buried in consecrated ground, but the parish priest would not allow it, presumably because her daughter had taken her own life. The girl's mother was consumed by guilt, and felt she had let her daughter down.

In fact, Spirit doesn't condemn those who take their own lives. There's no judgement there about how or why they passed over – whether through illness, accident or through choice.

'But mum, it doesn't matter where my bones go,' her daughter reassured her. 'Just put some flowers by my picture.' Her mother felt relieved to hear her daughter again, and so a little of her grief could begin to heal. I have seen this client regularly, and her daughter always comes through to comfort her.

September 11, 2001

After the September 11 terrorist attack, I felt such deep sorrow. I rarely cancel any appointments for readings, but during that week I simply had to. I didn't feel grief for those who had died, because they are now in spirit, but my heart went out to those left behind, because they are the ones who must live with their terrible loss. I prayed for them all, which was my way of sending healing to those so tragically bereaved. Like everyone else, I called all my friends in New York, trying to find out if they were OK. Unfortunately, several of my clients, who had become good friends, died as a result of the attack.

That week, two people in spirit woke me up during the night. I felt that they wanted to tell me what had happened to them. The first one came to talk to me three days after his death.

'I'm Connor,' he began. He told me that he had been working in the towers.

'I had moments of fear, only moments, then I was flying,' he related. He explained that the attack had happened so quickly: 'The plane came towards the office, flying level with the floor.' As the plane had hit, he told me that he had felt an explosion of air, and that the air was taken out of his body. He was still holding his telephone.

Another night that week, the second man came to tell me his story. He and the others had been stuck at the eighty-fifth floor in one of the towers. Everyone had assumed that a bomb had exploded, and they had no idea that the tower was about to collapse on top of them. He had been walking down the stairs, trying to get out. There were so many people that they were moving very slowly, and they were all scared. 'We felt that the building kept moving,' he told me, 'a slow movement, like a mudslide.' The windows were cracking. 'We were all saying, "We'll be OK as long as we keep going."' He said that one person began to talk about the party they were planning, to try to keep everyone believing they would see a future.

'Then we all held hands,' he continued. 'Someone started saying the Lord's Prayer, and a woman was singing.' Then – nothing. He had not felt anything as the weight of the building above had impacted upon them all.

'I didn't feel pain,' he said. 'I felt fear, but we were all frightened.'

One year on from September 11, I visited ground zero. There was such a sense of solitude and sadness there. As I looked over the site, I saw three people in spirit wandering around. One man was Oriental, and the other two Caucasian. All three were business people, standing there in their shirtsleeves. They were bewildered – they didn't feel dead, but they knew that they were. I felt that they had loved the twin towers and had really enjoyed working there. I knew that they had jumped from their offices, and had chosen not to die by fire. I talked to them internally, saying 'You can go home now. You don't have to stay here.' They did not acknowledge me although I did see them leave.

Listening to those in spirit who needed to tell me their stories, and acknowledging the presence of those three lost souls at ground zero, was the best healing I could give at the time. Even during an incident so horrific as September 11, there is always something you can do, no matter how small it may feel at the time. Your intention to help is always heard by Spirit.

To truly listen to others without wanting something in return is to give great healing.

Taking responsibility for your own healing

As we have seen, trapped emotions are often manifested as physical pain. If there's a conversation we need to have, and can't admit what we need to say to others or ourselves, it may fester and manifest as physical pain. This is because all our cells – not just our brain cells – have memories. Every cell within the body feels and remembers everything.

We need to learn to be honest with ourselves, and this can take courage. If you have a pain in your neck, you might consider that somebody else is literally being a pain, or that you may be the pain in the neck for someone else. When you feel pain, it doesn't always mean that you are the only one suffering it. Pain is another source of sensory information – it is the soul's way of communicating through the body. If you can be truly honest with yourself, you will see the cause of your pain and understand how it might be alleviated. When you take responsibility for yourself, your words and actions, you also take care of your body and soul.

When you are suffering pain, it can be hard to know how to help heal yourself. The pain interferes with your senses, because your focus is purely on the pain. For example, some people suffer constant pain, due to arthritis, migraines or constant back problems. But even when pain becomes familiar, you can work with it. If you can look inside yourself and understand the message that your pain is giving you about deeper life issues, you can ask the pain to leave you. You can simply decide that you don't want it. It's not about reasoning, or thinking to yourself, 'Look, I could do without this', but feeling: 'I really, *really* do not need this any longer'. It is that you have taken real notice of what is behind the pain, so you don't need the reminder any more. Then, when you can speak with truth from your soul, Spirit will hear and help you.

I discovered the truth of this when I suffered a serious illness in my thirties. When I became ill, I was not following my spiritual life path. Our catering business had collapsed because I had not followed my instinct on a business deal, and we had been defrauded. Also, in those days, I was not closely in touch with my guides on a daily basis. I had already met Li Ching (see page 44), but at this stage I wasn't doing readings, which was the work that I knew Spirit needed me to do. We were selling our house to pay business debts rather than go bankrupt, and were soon to be homeless. We had no money or business. Everything that had once been stable in life was being challenged, and it was such a miserable, stressful time.

I was sent to hospital with a headache so horrendous that my vision had become impaired. My head had been throbbing for two months, and I had very little eyesight. The scan showed a light patch on my brain – a sign that I had a growth. It was quite small, about half the size of my little fingernail. I was told to return to the hospital in eight weeks' time, when they would give me another scan. The thought of enduring that pain for another two months, or longer, was unbearable. I was exhausted and very depressed. I could hardly sleep because my head felt so huge. The shape of my face was altering, and the left side, where I felt the most pain, had begun to distort.

One afternoon, when the pain was particularly bad, I felt compelled to get out of the house. I set out towards the woods with Portia, my German shepherd dog. I could feel every footfall; every step I took reverberated in my head. It was excruciatingly painful, but I had to have some fresh air, and to get away from the house for a short while.

We must have walked for miles. Eventually, I found a resting place by a tree. I felt so desperate to be free of the pain that I banged my head on its trunk, trying to make my headache disappear. I actually wanted to feel a different kind of pain. I sat there and thought: 'Please God, take this headache away and I will do your work. I will do whatever you ask me to do, but you have to take this headache away, because I can't work with this.' Portia comforted me, nuzzling into my neck, and we stayed there for quite some time.

Slowly I stood up, and felt lighter. The pain was subsiding. As I walked back to the house, I realised that I couldn't feel my footfalls any longer, and by the time that I got home, most of the pain had gone.

I turned to my husband, Michael, and told him that God had healed me.

He looked at me, sceptically.

'But I asked God for healing,' I continued. 'I didn't mean to ask – I just did.'

I know that I was healed because I asked for healing from a place deep within me – from my heart and soul. I believe that when you truly ask from your soul, you do receive help. It's no good asking from what I call the 'surface', or your personality, because Spirit responds to your intention, not your language.

After three days, the pain had completely disappeared.

When I went back to the hospital, I knew that the growth had gone, but I didn't mention this to anyone other than my husband and children. I had a scan, and the radiographer returned with the results, looking slightly puzzled, and said that she needed to run the scan again. She did so, and I heard her discussing the results with the doctor. They then told me that the growth had gone. I said, 'God healed it.'

'It's true,' I continued. 'I asked God to heal it, and he did so, and I know when he took the growth away.'

They exchanged a glance that said, 'We've got a right one here!' I didn't mind this. It was more important to me to acknowledge, in public, what had taken place that day of the walk. I looked at the scan results for myself, together with the earlier scan. On the second scan there was only a tiny scratch, a cross. I know that this was the scar left by the pain of the headache. I believe that severe pain leaves a scar, and that it remains in the cellular tissue of our body and in the memory of our cells.

Since then, neither the growth nor the pain has returned. I kept my word to God, and I began by paying attention to my guidance once again. I realised, through my experience of pain and impaired sight, I needed to see things in a new light. My healing crisis was a wake-up call to remind me of my true purpose in life – reading for others. Running a catering business wasn't what Spirit had wanted me to do.

Remember to thank Spirit for their support and protection. They are guiding you with love.

THE EXERCISES

Whether you are healing yourself or others, always see the hope, the brightness, within you and those you want to heal. Trust in what you are trying to do, and in the guidance that is there to help you. You can call in your guides by name (see Chapter 2, page 53). Ask for whatever is needed. Put no limitations on the 'how' – just do what feels right at the time. Remember, you are the healing tool, the physical point of access to the recipient through which healing power can come through. Let go of conscious thought and just be in the moment. When you do this, you can let go of the outcome. Spirit knows what is needed.

When you ask for healing, ask for the cause of the ailment to be healed as well as the physical symptom.

1 Healing yourself

Healing yourself involves taking responsibility for your-self, your feelings and the healing process itself. This exercise will help you to tune in to the messages of your body.

1   Centre yourself by visualising a candle flame and cupping your hands around it. Keep seeing and feeling the warm light, then move your hands apart, expanding the light until you lose aware-ness of your hands (see page 32). Let the light become you – feel the glow inside you. Let it expand.

2   Say and feel your intention to receive healing. You can speak out loud or to yourself, but feel your wish deeply. Don't set any limits, or have an expectation about the kind of healing you'll expe-rience. If you have a specific complaint, you can visualise the area of pain in your body. You don't have to be anatomically exact.

3   Let your senses guide you. Let any feelings you have expand. You may receive a sensation on your skin, or visualise an image. Watch the intru-sion of your thoughts, and let them go. Just feel, and allow yourself to be completely open.

What did you sense?

Spirit may take you on an unexpected journey inside your body or mind to start or complete a healing task. This may feel like watching a science-fiction film – whatever it is, just go with it. Your inner, infinite wisdom may speak to you through images that they know you will understand, so the answers will become clear. You may travel through your body, without seeing anything change inside you. This in itself can signal the beginning of the process of healing. All you need do is observe yourself internally through the guidance of Spirit.

If you ask for help with a particular ailment, Spirit may show you images of everyday tools that will resonate with you. For example, if you had a growth in your body, you might be shown garden secateurs or a trowel, and feel that you want to imagine using one of them to cut or dig out the growth. You can experiment with your tools and find the best way to use them, guided by Spirit at every step.

2 Healing others: what kind of healer are you?

Healers can work in many different ways. For instance:

* **Speaking healers** are exceptional listeners. Their friends often confide in them, and they heal others through listening and talking. In my experience, if speaking healers have little opportunity to use their healing ability, they tend to suffer from terrific headaches caused by a build-up of tension in their bodies. By healing others through their words, their energy flows.

* **Touch healers** are naturally tactile. They can't help touching people they meet, almost as if they're using touch to punctuate their sentences. However, they also instinctively know when a person doesn't like being touched, and they will change their behaviour accordingly. Touch healers work by physically touching a person's skin or by working with their aura. If touch and auric healers don't use their energy for healing, I have found that they often suffer arm, shoulder or neck problems, again due to a build-up of energy in those areas.

* **Auric healers** work in a similar way to touch healer, except that they have no need for physical contact in order to heal. Instead, they work with

the energy of a person's aura which they will still use their hands to feel.

You can discover if you may heal by physical touch or auric contact by trying the following exercise:

1   Hold your hands about a shoulder-width apart. Sit very still, and focus your awareness on the palms of your hands.
2   Slowly move your palms towards each other. Pay attention to what you sense. If you feel a tingling in your palms, a sense of resistance or a change in air temperature, stop moving your hands. Otherwise, keep moving them. You may not feel anything until your palms touch.

What did you sense?

The point at which you felt sensation, such as resistance or tingling, is the distance from which you can heal. If you stopped moving your hands when they were four or so inches apart, then you are an auric healer. If you sensed something when your palms touched, you may heal by placing your hands on the recipient.

3 Healing through the aura or by physical contact

1 Bring your hands four inches or so from the recipient's body, so that you are in their auric field (see above).

2 Alternatively, lightly touch the recipient's hands or shoulders.

3 Allow healing energy to flow through you. Keep your mind out of the way. You are a clear and perfect channel for healing.

4 You may also be drawn to a particular part of the body. It may be hot or cold – go to it and stay for as long as you feel you need to.

4 Absent healing

If I am asked to send someone healing energy, I will always do this. Also, I have learned through my work with Spirit that other people can take healing from me – if they really need extra strength, they can visualise me and hook into my energy field.

For this exercise, it doesn't matter if you want to send healing to your neighbour or someone living on the other side of the world. The technique is always the same.

1　Sit comfortably, where you can be quiet and still.
2　Sense the person's name, face or voice. If you have a photograph of them, you can look at it, too.
3　Imagine that you are travelling to see the person who you want to heal. Visualise this as a light beam that takes you from your home to wherever they may be. You are there in an instant, bringing with you light energy.
4　Let your gift of light illuminate the person. See them flooded with healing light.
5　Let Spirit guide you to continue the light bath. Ask Spirit to send whatever healing is right for this person, through your conduit of light. If you want to ask Spirit to heal a specific ailment, ask them to do so.

6 When the healing has been sent, you need to heal the auric field around that person by visualising a large light around them.

7 Healing the aura protects them and seals in the healing, keeping it working after the visualisation. If you forget to do this, the benefits may not last and you will need to keep sending healing energy.

What did you sense?

You may have visualised the person's ailment during the healing. Did you see it disappear? You may have felt that you treated an ailment. For example, if I am shown a tumour, I look at it and send a laser beam to cauterise it. I see it turn to powder. I then visualise that person, happy and well.

When you send healing, don't attach yourself to a cure or an outcome. Believe in the process, then let go. You are sending healing through love, and that is enough.

4 Animal healing

Some sensitives have exceptional healing ability with animals. I once met a wonderful animal healer, Marian Evans, who healed a cat who had been run over by a car.

This cat had broken almost every bone in its body. The cat's owner told Marian that the vet had wanted to put her down, but instead she brought her pet to Marian. She told me that she hadn't known what to do about the cat's injuries, only that she had to act quickly. She laid her down on a rug in her bathroom. She went to her bedroom, and lay on her bed, wondering what she could do to heal the cat.

Spirit showed her a Ming vase, which had been shattered. She knew that she had to mentally retrieve every single piece, put it back in the correct place, and stick it together with whatever she could find. She started off by visualising toothpaste, then some glue, which she experimented with. This glue wasn't quite right, so she visualised another type of glue. She knew that she had to ensure that the surface of the repaired vase was smooth, so in her mind she smoothed her home-made mortar as she pieced together the vase. When she had finished her porcelain jigsaw and smoothed every rough edge, she drifted off to sleep.

In the morning, she awoke and went to use the bathroom, forgetting that she had laid the cat down there. She opened the door and the cat came running out – completely healed.

Chapter 5

Past Lives

Our soul holds the memory of every lifetime; it is your complete archive of living – past and present. There is a growing awareness by some people of what I call 'soul homesickness'. This is a need to remember our soul's journey. We may experience this as flashes of past lives. We are not shown past lives for fun – there is always a reason. When we remember and take notice of these moments, we are beginning our memory retrieval. This can show us how we may heal a situation in our life, and the information can help us to do this.

I do not profess to be a past-life therapist. What I do, with the help from my spirit friends, is to sense clients' past-life experiences, in order to help them move forward in their lives. I may sense these as a series of flashes, or I may actually slip into being that person in their past life.

A past-life situation can often explain the root cause of a problem. These can include relationship problems and behavioural issues such as bullying, eating disorders and obsessive cleanliness. Some clients experiencing these patterns have used this knowledge of their past life in counselling or psychotherapy.

An A-list Hollywood actor came to see me for what he described as 'a voyage into me': a way to find out if a past life had a bearing on his relationship patterns. At the time of his first visit, he had been married and divorced four times. His relationships usually ended due to his well-publicised affairs.

I looked into his past lives to see if I could help him.

I found myself in an Arab-style tent, talking with a small group of other men. I felt the weight of heavy jewellery on me, and I knew that I had power; it felt as if I were a tribal leader. I could see that I was wearing a decorative dagger, inlaid with what looked like rubies.

The conversation concerned a man whom I loved like a brother, who was to be killed as a punishment for his crime. I had a strong feeling that he had defiled a woman; I may have sensed this word from the men's talk, but what I felt outweighed any language. I wanted to scream inside, because I didn't want my friend to die. I couldn't save him, because to do so would have made me seem weak. The pain was unbearable, and I couldn't show it or do anything.

When I told my client about what I had experienced, we talked about his destructive behaviour with his previous wives. Losing his 'brother' in a past life had showed him the danger of getting too close to anyone, so in this life he chose to sabotage an otherwise happy relationship by having affairs. He admitted that one of his ex-wives had been the love of his life, but he had let her slip through his fingers because he couldn't deal with the intimacy. In his mind, he had to reject her before she rejected him. In this way, he felt that the circumstances of one of his past lives had shown him a way forward.

Several years after this reading, the client formed a much more positive relationship with a new partner. He continues to work with a trained past-life therapist to clear his past issues, and has made real progress in breaking a pattern that had hurt both himself and others.

*Any negative patterns in your relationships
are soul lessons that you can learn. Pay
attention to them.*

One regular client of mine is a well-known
designer. He has earned much recognition for his
work, but he came to see me because he felt
trapped by his own behaviour. He was obsessively
clean, washing his hands constantly. If someone
else took a tissue from his box, he would have to
throw the box away. He would only eat in the best
restaurants where the staff laid out a fresh towel for
each customer. In fact, anything touched just the
once by him or by someone else caused 'contami-
nation'. He was worried that in a past life he had
committed a terrible crime, and he'd almost convinced himself that he must have had blood on his
hands – and was paying the price in this life with
his obsession. He told me that when he washed his
hands, it felt as if he wanted to take off a layer of
skin, scrubbing until he felt that he could stop –
until the next time.

I asked Spirit to show me the cause of his behaviour.

The air was hot and dry, and the landscape felt for-
eign to me. My first sense was the stench of decaying
flesh. My skin was crawling, and I felt grey; I didn't

know if this was dirt or disease, or both. I was an Asian man, and there was something wrong with my body. I was misshapen. I touched my face, which was rough and lumpy.

I noticed that two or three others who stood nearby had the same complaint. We were lepers, outcasts, and everyone avoided us. I saw an area of low ground, and a natural cave in a rock face. I knew that I lived there with the others, and that people would throw food there for us to eat.

This was a living death, and I was unclean.

As I was speaking, I had my eyes closed. When I stopped talking, I opened them to see that my client was crying.

'When you were in my past life, I could see where you were before you described it,' he said tearfully. The recognition of his past life was very strong in him. 'And I had a distinctive flavour in my mouth, when you were telling me about being thrown food,' he continued. 'It was an odd sort of taste; maybe a kind of bread, but stale and gritty.'

He looked at me. 'It wasn't my fault, was it?'

'No, it wasn't,' I reassured him.

'It's just that I've always felt so guilty, needing to be clean and not wanting other people to touch things,' he confided.

This client is having psychotherapy to work through his behavioural pattern. We keep in touch, and he's making good progress. He still doesn't like anyone touching the rim of his cup – it must be held out to him by the handle – but little by little, he is learning to manage his obsession by under-standing the trauma of his past life. Feeling guilty doesn't always mean we are to blame.

Another client came to me to find out about his past life, because he too couldn't understand the cause of his obsessive behaviour – he had to keep washing his feet and changing his socks up to three or four times a day.

Spirit showed me one of his past lives.

My first impression was the smell of fermenting fruit. I looked around me, and sensed that I was in some kind of street market, or a road enclosed by houses. It wasn't a square. It was noisy, and bar-rows were rolling past me; their flat tops, which had odd-looking handles affixed to them, were piled with fruit and vegetables. I could see huge, metal-rimmed wheels turning. The wheels seemed large because I was small. I was a boy, dressed in scruffy-looking clothes, but I didn't feel hungry or unhappy. I was wearing shoes, yet my feet were freezing cold. How come I could feel the ground beneath me, when I had shoes on?

I realised then that I was wearing shoe uppers, but they had no soles left to speak of. I knew that my mother and father didn't have any money to spare, and they couldn't afford proper shoes for me. But they wanted me to look reasonable on the outside, although my bare feet were damp and dirty from walking the streets.

I told this to my client, who proceeded to show me his shoes. They had the thickest soles, which he told me he wore even in summer. He admitted that he couldn't go barefoot – even on a beach – or walk on the carpet inside his own home without shoes and socks on.

He felt relieved that we had found the cause of his problem, because he had not been able to stop blaming himself for not being able to understand or control his obsession with his feet. By recognising his past-life situation, he was able to feel less controlled by it. He still likes to change his socks and wear thick-soled shoes, but it's no longer a compulsion. He has a choice.

This next past-life experience was exceptionally vivid, and it came about because the client, a woman, had asked for help with her weight problem. She had been feeling depressed, and couldn't control her overeating. She had tried hypnotherapy, but with no success. Her obsession with food had begun in childhood, and it was now damaging her relationship with her husband and children.

Spirit answered by showing me a stone within her heart. This represented her loneliness. They then took me into her past life.

I was in a small country town. The air felt damp, although I knew that it hadn't been raining. The dampness and cold were within me. I looked down at myself; I was a child. I was dirty, and my sleeves were long and frayed. I think I was a boy, because my trousers were far too big for me. They felt rough against my skin. I wore odd shoes and they didn't fit. I was walking with one foot on the kerb and one in the gutter. I could hear my feet scraping over the cobblestones, and I saw that someone had tipped water into the gutter. Maybe I was trying to clean my shoes in the water.

I was starving hungry. I had an orange in my pocket, which I knew I had stolen.

I told my client the little boy's story: that he had been an orphan, sometime in the eighteenth century, and had had to fend for himself all his life. He had always been hungry, and never had much to eat. Even when he managed to get a little money, he still stole his food. He had lived until around thirty – a reasonable age given his impoverished circumstances.

The client showed me inside her coat pocket. Where the lining was torn, she had secreted two packets of sweets – hiding away the food she'd bought for herself like a thief. She told me that she was always worried that there would never be enough. Before eating all the food in the house, she would hide extra supplies for later, although she certainly didn't need to. Her behaviour was alienating her family, causing constant arguments at home.

As soon as I told her the story of her past life, she said that it resonated strongly within her. She knew that it was right. I always say to people, 'Just because I have said it, doesn't mean you have to believe it. If it doesn't feel right, don't accept it.' She took the tape of the reading home with her, and played it to her husband and children. They too recognised that the poverty of her past life was still playing a part in the present, and began to understand her eating problem. From that time onwards, she found it easier to trust that she would have food, and in time the weight came off. She stopped bingeing and hoarding, and now she's much slimmer – and happier with herself.

When we look back into another life, we need to do it with a purpose. Exploring past lives may appear to some people as a way to pursue their curiosity or ego: how many times have we heard people say, 'I wonder who I was?' With this usually comes the fantasy that they were Cleopatra or King Arthur, rather than the probability that they were peasants, foot soldiers, seamstresses or even prostitutes. Status is unimportant. Just as with spirit guides, what matters is what we can learn from a past experience. The question, really, should be 'Is my problem due to a past-life memory?' As we have seen, information about a past life can help you to break unhappy patterns of behaviour, empowering you to move on with your present life more successfully.

One client was indeed convinced that he had been King Arthur in a past life, and he came to me for confirmation. So I asked Spirit, and they said: 'We'll show you.'

I saw the client during the time of King Arthur. He was a foot soldier, and certainly not a king. I knew that he would feel deflated by this information, so I asked Spirit,

'What shall I tell him?'

'Tell him that he was a foot soldier in the time of King Arthur, and that he was a man who had done good things,' they replied.

My client wasn't happy with this. He seemed like a nice man, but he had a sense of self-importance.

'Are you sure?' he bristled. 'Wasn't I even an officer?' He didn't want to accept what I had told him, and I felt his frustration.

I looked into his previous life again, and saw him as a regular soldier. He was haranguing a fellow soldier, and I could sense how much the entire company disliked him.

He had come into his present lifetime assuming that he knew everything. I could feel his energy – and that he was thinking that I was talking utter rubbish. He seemed like the kind of person who needed absolute proof that I was telling him the truth.

Spirit showed me his past life for the third time. He and the other soldiers were outdoors. It was muddy and cold, and the company was tired and moaning about that evening's lookout duty. My client, however, was trying to push another man into taking his watch. This soldier had already taken his turn the previous night, but my client clearly thought that lookout duty was below him, and that this minion should do his work for him.

He was arrogant and bullying, and I relayed every word of the conversation between him and his victim. I looked at him and saw a stab of recognition: finally, Spirit had his attention.

'You have just described, almost word for word, a conversation that I have just had with my teenage son,' he explained. 'He's been bullying other children at school, and he won't obey me. I can't get him to conform.'

'I know I haven't told you about that conversation,' he continued. 'If I hadn't heard you say that with my own ears, I would never have believed it.'

He relaxed then, and started to talk to me. He agreed that he could be a bit of a bully; he worked as a teacher, and admitted that he demanded constant attention and obedience – not just from his pupils, but also from his long-suffering colleagues. But now he was seeing his own son copy his intimidating behaviour.

'Why am I still doing it?' he asked.

'Because you're not listening to yourself,' I replied. 'If you listened to yourself, you would really hear some of the hurtful things you say to others.'

Later, this man decided to have counselling and psychotherapy. I still see him, and he is now training to be a psychotherapist. He hopes to work with teenagers and possibly drug users. Spirit helped him to see his behaviour clearly, and from this he has made some positive decisions. He's still sometimes a little arrogant, but now he's prepared to listen to others. Knowledge of one of his past lives has helped him look at a negative pattern and find a way to move away from it.

Bullying was also the reason that the mother of a young girl first contacted me. She had a real problem with her child, who was seven or eight years old at the time, because she had found out that she was bullying other children at school. This girl had four brothers and sisters, and there was no bullying at home. Her mother couldn't comprehend why her daughter should be doing this. She was also embarrassed about her child's behaviour – she and her husband were both school teachers.

I didn't sense anything immediately that would explain why the girl was a bully. As her mother sat in front of me, I 'scanned' her daughter from a distance – I do this by seeing her in my mind's eye. I asked Spirit, 'Where does this behaviour come from?' I saw the girl, standing with hand on hip and her expression impassive. 'I'm not telling you anything,' she said. I had a deep sense that her bullying was not of this lifetime. Her mother had also told me how this girl hated to be touched by other children, and I felt that this physical contact was triggering a past-life memory. I asked Spirit to take me to the source of the problem.

The stench of excrement and human bodies made me feel nauseous. I looked at my body and saw that I had black skin. I knew that I was a slave, chained to other slaves by my feet and neck. I wore a hard metal torque around my neck, and the weight of a rope cut into my shoulder. The anklets had just a couple of links between them, so I could hardly move my feet. I didn't know where I was, only that there was a lot of wood around me, which looked bleached by the sun. I may have been on a ship, but I didn't feel its movement through the water.

I felt a searing pain on my arm and part of my back, and when I looked round I saw that I was being whipped, the lashes slicing deep into my skin. My captor had skin like me, and I remember seeing a white face, too. I knew that I was being punished for speaking up for someone else.

I talked about what I had seen with the girl's mother. To me, it felt as if her daughter was bullying other children as a pre-emptive measure, in case others would try to bully her first and the pattern would be repeated all over again. The girl's parents took her to a therapist, whom they told about her past life. Together, as they all worked on understanding the reason for her bullying, her behaviour towards other children became more positive. She's since grown up to be a very independent woman and her ambition is to be a barrister, speaking up for other people.

Non-judgement

Non-judgement is vital in the work that I do. When you see someone in a damaging relationship, for example, it may be that they are learning a soul lesson: they will leave that relationship when they are ready to move on. They decide, not anyone else. Everything in life can teach us things that we need to know. We experience all things for a reason.

THE EXERCISES

When you access a past life, your aim should be to heal an existing negative pattern of behaviour in your life. Try not to use the experience as an excuse to hold you back. By this I mean that some people can regard it as 'fate' that they are, for example, addicted to gambling, compulsively jealous, self-sabotaging or violent, because they discovered this pattern of behaviour in their experience of a previous life. Use the knowledge of your past to go forward and bring out the best in yourself. Forgive the past. Be aware of it – just don't dwell there. Let the past be your healer, not your jailer.

It is also important to bear in mind that accessing a past life can bring up other issues or insights that you were not expecting. Trust that whatever else arises in these exercises is right for you at the time.

Take your time. Don't rush. You can come out of a journey at any point that you choose. It is a positive journey, and there is nothing to fear.

1 Accessing your spiritual memories

Childhood spiritual memories are a part of your soul memory. Children remember far more of their past lives than adults. In this exercise, you can journey back to childhood to access your memories of past lives in a safe way.

1 Find a peaceful and quiet place.
2 Visualise the protective light cocoon (*see* page 68).
3 Visualise a flower: look at its form, colour and texture.
4 Open the centre of the flower to reveal a path that leads way off into the distance. The path leads downwards. The sun is shining very brightly.
5 Look for a gate and go through it. Know it is the gate to all the good memories that you hold of your past.
6 See yourself, as a child sitting somewhere that is safe and beautiful.
7 Now let your memories of spirit come back to you. Don't judge, just go with what you see and experience.
8 Stop when you feel you want to – don't tire yourself. Remember, you can leave the journey at any time.

What did you sense?

What did your body tell you during the exercise? Did you feel relaxed as you looked at your flower? Did you feel calm and happy? Pay attention to everything that you sensed. Make notes of what you experienced.

2 Looking at life's patterns

You can practise this exercise at the end of each day to help increase your awareness of negative and positive patterns of behaviour.

1 Put your light cocoon around your body (*see* page 68).
2 Consider all the events of the day and remember all the situations that arose.
3 Call your friends from the spirit world and ask them to help you to look in depth and understand your day from their perspective. Ask to see where you are caught in negative patterns and where you acted with positivity and love.
4 Do not analyse; just allow the awareness to seep into you.
5 Resolve to integrate this awareness into your everyday life. Give yourself a time at the end of each day to find time to sit quietly in the stillness.

What did you sense?

Take notice of the very first feelings you felt – not what you'd like to feel – as these are the true answers to your life at present. Remember that information may come through any sense; sometimes you may hear something, or hear internally when you get a strong sense of knowing inside.

3 Accessing a past life

This is a technique, taught to me by Spirit, which you can use to go back into past-life situations.

1 Sit quietly with both feet on the ground. Make sure you're warm and comfortable, and that you won't be disturbed.

2 Protect yourself by visualising your light cocoon (*see* page 68): let white light encircle your whole body, from your toes to your head, and seal it at the top, above your crown.

3 Now open your first five chakras, by seeing a flower opening for each one (see page 33). At the third chakra, you'll dive into a volcano of cool or warm liquid gold, and shower under stardust. This gives you energy and protection.

4 Open the sixth chakra. See the petals of your flower opening, feeling their texture and energy. Look into the centre of the flower – it is widening, so you can move through it. The flower disappears, and you'll see marble stairs leading down. Walk down the stairs, moving deeper into the depths of your own chakra. It's not dark down there – light is streaming in on you from above. Look around as you go.

5 At the foot of the stairs, you'll see a large door. The word 'Truth' appears over it. Open the door, and enter the room beyond.

6 There is a mirror to your left, which represents the past. Look into it. Ask to see the past life that will help you with your present dilemma or pattern. Don't have any expectation. Trust that you will be shown what you need to see.

7 Now step through the mirror into a past life. You can keep stepping through the mirror to access more past lives. The mirror represents infinity.

8 When you are ready, step back from the mirror and close your chakras. Do this by visualising two flaps for each chakra, one inside the other. You opened six chakras during this exercise, so close the flaps six times.

If you like, you can write down what you witnessed as you may soon forget the detail.

What did you sense?

Did you see anything in the mirror? Don't analyse what you did, or didn't see. Again, you will be shown what is needed now, to help you go forward in the present. If you did see yourself in a past life, how did this feel? Status isn't important; it's the sense of yourself in the past that matters. For example, you may have seen a well-dressed person, but how did it make you feel, seeing him or her? Pay attention to your senses, not your assumptions about how you might have lived.

The journey of the soul

Part of our reason for living in this life is to retrieve your soul memory, and use it to be the best you can in this life. When you are at your best, you can continue the life path you created for yourself when you were between earthly lives. You created this life path because of the lessons you need to learn. When a person has lived out all of their life's lessons, there is no need for them to return to Earth, and their journey is complete. They can return to Earth again if they so choose, or may stay in the spirit world, becoming a guardian angel for a new-born child. A person's guardian angel stays with them throughout their lifetime.

While an old or evolved soul eventually goes 'home' or back to spirit, a young soul has many lifetimes to live out. I think of a young soul as someone who has experienced fifteen to twenty lifetimes. I often recognise young souls because they tend toward a teenage mentality, even throughout the later stages of their earthly life. They may hold quite narrow views and appear dogmatic – they need to be right! Their heads rule their hearts, and results matter. Their surroundings, too, are not so important to them. A young soul may lack sensitivity because they have not yet evolved through the experience of many lifetimes. Young souls are not bad people, however; they are just at a different stage of their soul journey. Everything comes at its right time in our soul's journey.

People can stay in spirit for as long as they choose to. They may reincarnate after a few years, but many stay in order to greet their loved ones when they pass over, or until they are sure that their loved ones on Earth are alright. They progress in spirit as we progress during our lives; they journey with us.

Some people in spirit may partly incarnate into a new spirit, or baby, so they simultaneously exist in spirit and on Earth. When the person in spirit decides to fully incarnate into a living individual, the spirit and soul integrate. When people say, 'she's truly come into her own', for me it can often mean the completion of one cycle of the soul's journey.

Chapter 6

Talking with Animals

As a child, I was always aware that animals had things to say to each other. I once overheard a company of frogs talking amongst themselves, their repetitive little voices as human as a conversation in the school playground. I told a friend about it, who replied, 'How do you know it's not just your imagination?'

'Because there were so many of them,' I explained. Fifty or so frogs had been migrating across the road, presumably on a pilgrimage to the nearby stream to lay their spawn. To my ears their loud, incessant chatter – 'I'm in a hurry', 'Move over, move over!' – was unmistakable. Yet I didn't really think that this was so unusual; I was already talking with my spirit guides by then, so why wouldn't animals talk, too?

Throughout my life I have heard and talked with cats, dogs, horses, cows and even ants, both here and in spirit. Like us, all animals have energy fields (the etheric, auric and emotional fields – *see* page xxx). When animals return in spirit, just like humans they use their etheric energy field (the closest to the physical body) in order to take their original form, which is why in a reading they appear to me as they usually looked when they were living. The returning spirit energy of a deceased animal is as strong as that of a person in spirit, and these animals always come back with love. They also know how much you loved them in life, as animals interact with us at the level of heart and soul.

Animals undoubtedly have souls. Their spirituality has been celebrated in ancient and contemporary culture, from the cat revered by Egyptian society to the sacred cow of Hinduism. Our childhood storybooks have taught us about the wisdom of the owl, the endurance of the tortoise, the loyalty of the dog. Our relationship with animals is part of our ancestral inheritance, and the companionship we share with them continues after death. In spirit, animals and people continue to inhabit the same world.

In readings, people in spirit often bring their beloved spirit animals with them. During a reading for one lady, her husband in spirit came through with his little dog. When he had been a boy of seven or eight years old, he had taken in an unwanted Collie cross – the runt of a litter. He had adored his new dog, who comforted him whenever he had felt frightened, and particularly when his father's unpredictable temper let fly. On one occasion, after another of the father's outbursts, the dog bit the older man to protect his master. Furious, he beat the puppy so severely that the vet had had to amputate one of his legs. The boy wouldn't allow his pet to be put down, so he saved up all his pocket money and did odd jobs for the local farmers in order to afford the vet's bills.

The dog survived for seven years, until the boy turned fourteen. He had been able to keep one precious photograph of his dog, which he had hidden on the back of his headboard. It was the only place that he could keep it safe from his father, who had torn up all his other pictures.

It due course, he grew up and married, always treasuring the memory of his dog – and the one photograph, which passed to his wife after he died.

When I read for this lady, I saw her husband and his dog together in spirit. I was told that the dog had waited for his master, or 'Dad', and he showed himself with all his legs. She was moved to hear that her husband had finally been reunited with his beloved best friend.

Animals naturally understand our emotions. Our pets will always want to be close to us if we are in distress.

One female client had married a man who loved cats. During the reading, a grey Siamese cat with brown-tipped ears appeared and sat proudly between her feet.

She began to sneeze, and the cat cried, 'That's because of me!'

After we had finished the reading, she said, 'I don't know what's making me sneeze. I must have a cold coming on.'

'There was a cat sitting with you.'

'I'm allergic to cats,' she admitted. 'But only if they sit on my lap, or rub against me.' She thought that I was talking about one of my cats, so she looked under her chair and around the room, but she couldn't see anything. My animals had not been in my reading room.

I explained that I was referring to a cat in spirit. I told her the cat's name, which was Maya, and she was astounded. This was confirmation that her husband's old Siamese had indeed paid her a visit.

'But why me?' she asked. 'I like cats, but this one wasn't particularly close to me.'

'She wanted to bring her love to your husband, through you,' I explained.

Some more unusual pets come back from spirit to be with their owners. During a reading for one client, I saw a little yellow snake slither around her arm and put its head on her shoulder. I couldn't quite believe what I was seeing, but I accepted it and carried on.

The snake then asked me if I was going to talk about him.

'Do you belong to her?' I queried.

'Of course I do!' he replied. I asked Spirit if this lady might be pleased to hear about the snake, and they told me 'yes'. So I took a deep breath.

'I can see a snake on your arm.'

'What does it look like?'

'He's small and yellow,' I began. 'He's a funny little thing, really, with no teeth. He's really happy.'

She was surprised and delighted to hear about him. She told me that his name had been Corker, and that she had loved him very much.

'Tell her that I chose her, and she will know what you are talking about,' Corker instructed. The lady then said that she had found Corker living in a house that she had moved into. He had hidden himself from his previous owners, but showed himself to her when she had arrived. They had lived together for many years.

Speaking with animals in this life

I know that animals have far more understanding of us than we have of them. We may train our animals to do specific tasks, but mostly they train us. By being close to animals and observing their behaviour in greater detail, we can learn their language.

I always try to speak from my heart, not my head: the head talks at, whereas the heart talks to. Animals are calm by nature, so communicating with them from my heart, with feeling, mirrors their relaxed sensibility. I often talk to my own animals internally, rather than out loud. I tell them what I'll be doing – if I'm going upstairs, for example, I tell them that I'll be there. When I'm away from home, I talk to them every day. I don't always hear what they are saying, but quite often I do.

Although I had overheard animal conversations many times during my childhood, an animal had not spoken to me directly until my puppy, Kahn, was hit by a motorbike. Through this tragic episode, I got back in touch with my ability to communicate with animals, just as I could talk with my spirit guides. Before his death, Kahn told me that he was dying in words that were so painfully audible to me: 'But mummy, you didn't tell me that it would hurt so much.' He had the pure voice of a child, and I felt as if one of my children were speaking to me. Although he had been hit by a motorbike, he had run back to me without any visible sign of injury. I checked his gums and realised that he was bleeding internally, so we drove him to the vet's surgery. I looked into his eyes and I know that I heard his voice again: 'Don't come in, mummy, because

I won't come out.' I stood outside in tears. In my mind, I said goodbye to him, and felt his spirit leave his body as he passed away.

After that incident, I started talking with animals much more. I'd say hello to cats and dogs in passing, and if I need an animal to do something, I'll ask (*see* page 199 for more on making requests to animals).

A family friend was very concerned about her dog's health, because she was refusing to eat or drink. I went to see her with my daughter, Tanya, and first of all I asked her dog if I could talk to her to find out the cause of her distress. Animals always self-diagnose; they know what is wrong with them.

She explained that she had eaten something bad on the beach. She was a puppy at the time, and hadn't realised that she had ingested poison, possibly from oil or tar. This substance had caused blisters in the lowest part of her throat. 'That's why I can't eat or drink,' she said. My daughter held her and gave her healing, and I asked the puppy what she thought would help her.

'Milk and bread would suit me,' she said.

I talked to her owner, and relayed to her what had been said. She then told me that she had already taken the dog to see a vet, who suspected that she had been poisoned. However, she couldn't afford the fees for further tests.

We fed her puppy on the milk and bread that she had asked for, and she soon recovered her strength.

I love horses. Many times, friends of mine who keep horses have asked me for help in diagnosing their animal's illness, often when a horse is not responding to treatment. I was asked to talk to a very distressed mare, who was being aggressive towards her owners. No one could understand why – she was healthy and comfortable, and had the companionship of other animals around her.

After asking if it was OK to talk with her, I questioned her about her behaviour.

'What's wrong?'

'I was starved by my previous owners,' she replied. 'So I have to eat up all my food very quickly. They come to feed me, and I barge them out of the way after they've put my feed down.'

I talked to the owner, who explained that this was exactly what the mare had been doing. It had become almost impossible to approach her, although she obviously wanted her feed. I went to talk to her again.

'What can we do to help? I asked. 'Because the people here want to help you.'

'They need to give me food more often,' she replied. 'I want to graze all the time; I don't want my bowl to be empty.'

The empty bowl reminded her of her starvation. We did what she asked, and she was fed three or four times a day rather than the usual two times. The next week saw a transformation in her behaviour as she began to feel more secure about being fed, and in turn her manner towards her owners and stable hands became more relaxed and much less aggressive.

Michael, a friend of mine, breeds Arab horses. At his stud farm are over one hundred mares and stallions, which included one stunning mare named Holly Blue. She was *grande dame* to all the horses there, so Michael was very concerned when she fell ill. Knowing that I talked with animals, he called me to see if there was anything that I could do to help Holly Blue. Her vet had been treating her with homeopathic and conventional medicines, but she wasn't showing any signs of recovery. He had known Holly Blue since she was a foal, and was doing everything he could to save her. I didn't know the nature of Holly Blue's illness at that stage, and I decided to hear it from the horse's mouth, so to speak. I decided to talk to her first before talking with the vet, who was up at Michael's house at that time. Having visited the farm many times before, I knew where Holly Blue was stabled.

I approached her, and gently stroked her face. She was a magnificent animal, grey with white freckles over her face like snowflakes. I asked her what the matter was.

'It's in my gut, I've got a blockage. It's all twisted,' she said.

'Can we put this right?' I asked. Holly Blue said we might, but that she wasn't sure.

'What do you need?'

'I need fluids.'

I went to the vet, and told him about this conversation. Michael had already explained to him that I talked with animals, so there was no issue about what I was trying to do – we both wanted the best for Holly Blue. The symptoms she had described to me matched the vet's diagnosis of acute colic. She had suffered from this condition previously and had recovered, he explained, but now he was deeply concerned that she might not survive this time around. We gave her more fluids, as she had requested. At that point, she told me that she was in terrible pain.

I stayed with her for a long time that November evening, stroking her mane as the rain pounded the stable roofs. Holly Blue then told me that it was her time to go.

The vet examined her again. Michael, the vet, my daughter Tanya, the head groom Sasha, the stable hands and I all knew that she would have to be put down, but no one wanted to say it. She was so beautiful – she had even been presented to the Queen earlier that year. Most of all, the horses in the stalls closest to her knew that she would die, too. As we began to walk her out of the stable into the yard, the horses began to lick the air.

'What are they doing?' I asked Holly Blue.

'They are saying, "Farewell",' she replied.

As we passed the other stables, all the horses put their heads over their stalls, then promptly turned their backs on her. This is a salute, a mark of respect from one animal to another. Animals give each other and their human companions dignity in death. I felt Holly Blue communing with the other horses as over one hundred of them, including her own foal, stood silently to pay tribute – no shuffling of hooves, or neighing; just a deep, deep silence.

We walked her towards the paddock in front of the house, where the vet was to give her an injection.

I felt very sad that this magnificent horse was going to die. I could have decided to leave Holly Blue then, because I felt so distraught, but I wanted to be with her.

'I am brave; I'm not afraid. I'm happy to be going where I'm going,' she told me. She was almost saying this to reassure myself and the others. Her voice was absolutely clear, and I felt no doubt about what I had heard.

The vet administered the injection; everyone else turned away, but I just couldn't. She closed her eyes and swallowed and, as she exhaled, a brilliant white light emanated from her body. I watched, transfixed, as the light took the form of a new-born foal, her legs folded under her stomach. This little blue-white spirit horse, this magical creature of fairy tale, stood before me. She shook her mane and streaked up to the sky like a firework. Now she was a point of light, a tiny, distant star in the night. I had just witnessed a spirit leaving a body, reborn to pass from this life into the spirit realm. I pointed to the light and exclaimed to the others, but they looked and didn't see Holly Blue.

I realised then that I couldn't feel the rain running over my skin. The rain had stopped and, just as we were about to turn back to the house, a shooting star glittered through the night sky. The stillness was absolute as we all looked upwards. 'Look,' my friend smiled, 'Holly Blue's a shooting star.'

There was no sound from the other horses, but I felt they all knew the moment of her passing. All the horses mourned her that night, and I was privileged to have seen her spirit at the moment of her death.

On my journey back home, I saw two more shooting stars; we rarely see them in England in November. For me, it was the third sign of Holly Blue's ascent to spirit.

The next day, she was buried in the bluebell wood near her home. For several days afterwards, none of the other horses would return to the paddock where Holly Blue died. I went up to the farm, and left some flowers for her at the gate. This was my way of saying goodbye.

Holly Blue has talked to me since her death, and I know that she is happy and free from pain.

THE EXERCISES

Animals will know if you are genuine about communicating with them. For example, if you're petting someone else's cat or dog because you feel you have to, but you don't feel anything for them, the animal will walk away. They respond according to the truth of your emotions.

By listening to animals, rather than scolding them, you can also discover the reasons for their behaviour. If your dog keeps rolling in mud, he can tell you that it's because his fur itches; if a cat needs to dig in the garden, she may tell you that it's because she is following a scent.

When you speak to animals from the heart, and with respect for their dignity, you can begin to communicate – to listen and to talk. You may also ask them to do something for you.

1 Communicating with animals

When you look into an animal's eyes, you may get a sense of what he or she is communicating. However, do not stare at an animal, as they will see this as confrontational.

1 Imagine that you are the animal you want to talk to.
2 Be still in your mind. Ask the animal if they will talk to you.
3 At first, they may just look at you, and you may feel a sense of understanding with each other. You may sense what they are saying, without mentally hearing them. When you have established an understanding, they will speak to you.
4 Ask them what they need you to know. They won't engage in idle chatter!
5 Practise talking to the animal without speaking out loud.
6 Remember not to prejudge what will be said. Let an understanding evolve between you.
7 Most of all, feel love for and honour the animal; they will know it when you don't.

What did you sense?

You may have heard a clear voice, or got a sense of the animal's voice as an internal vibration. This feels like a thought on the inside, which becomes an understanding.

2 Requesting an animal to do something

When you ask an animal to do something, it is vital that you afford that animal complete respect. You are asking, not ordering, them to co-operate. You may ask in any situation – and it doesn't matter if you don't already know the animal. Here's an example.

One night at home I was planning a party on the veranda, but the place was swarming with ants – there were literally hundreds of them. So I went to see if I could communicate with them.

'You're invading my space,' I began, 'and you can't stay here, because if you stay, you will die.' They would be so easily trampled on by the guests I was expecting. I advised them to find somewhere else in my garden, and I promised them that they would not knowingly be disturbed.

'You've got fifteen minutes if you understand our time,' I said.

I returned to the veranda five minutes later – and they had all disappeared. In the four years that we lived in that house, the ants didn't return.

When you genuinely explain the reason for your request, animals will hear you. Like spirit guides, animals respond to the genuine intent behind your words, not the words themselves.

Where Do You Go from Here?

I wrote this book primarily because Spirit asked me to, and the time also felt right to share some of my knowledge and experiences with others. It is my hope that, having read the book and followed the exercises, you will take this further and develop your senses as part of your daily life. If you aim to do the full chakra exercises at least once every other week, you will develop your senses even further. At the end, take notes and see how, with each journey, you are able to sense so much more – and more easily. Repeat the exercises until you feel comfortable and familiar with being guided. Remember, answers to specific questions often come from inside yourself – a voice from within, or sensing the answer with a deep knowing. Sometimes an answer, when realised, will bring you a smile of recognition. This is your higher self revealing the answers that have always been within you.

Being psychic, or sensitive, does not mean that you have to read for others. The aim of this book is to help you use your sensitivity with your psychic ability in your daily life, have a greater understanding of yourself and others, be more aware of your surroundings, of sounds, of the beauty and perfume of plants, and enrich your life. Don't limit yourself, and you will have a far greater appreciation of everything in this world.

Yes, you are psychic. Now use this ability spiritually. Spirituality is a way of being: always trying to treat others as you would have them treat you. Speak with truth from your heart, and try not to be judgemental of others. Do not strive to be a 'do-gooder', but instead just be yourself, with all your flaws (we all have them). Everyday, try to be the best that you can be, whatever your circumstances present you with. If you have to deal with difficult people at home or at work, send them a prayer of love, one that could help that person find love in themselves so that they can love others. Then move on, and avoid dwelling on their issues – you have enough of your own to deal with. Don't overload yourself.

As time goes on, you will discover a gradual change in yourself as you come into your own truths. In many gentle ways, your inner strength and courage will support you more and more through your increasing sensitivity. The more you accept what is happening, the stronger it will become. You will also find the right people come into your life to help you. Speak truthfully and the knowledge will increase and you will find abundance in all parts of your life. It doesn't happen all at once – it is a gradual awakening to the wonder of this multi-dimensional world we inhabit with so many unseen friends. When you are truly in rhythm with Spirit, you will find a peace inside you that emanates like a warm, shining smile. You will then be your own true light, sparkling for all to see.

Remember, faith and trust are just two sides of the same coin. You cannot have one without the other.

Enjoy your journey, and use your gifts to enhance your life.

May your guardian angel take you further than your dreams.

Dorothy, with love.

The Spiritual Journey

Dorothy Chitty

This CD guides you deep into the chakras, helping you to develop and expand your own spiritual knowledge. The meditation forms the basis of Dorothy's teachings.

Guided by Dorothy's gentle voice, you will become more aware of your senses, through the teaching of Spirit, and discover the difference between your thoughts and your spirit speaking.

This CD is available through Dorothy's websites: www.dorothychitty.co.uk or www.dorothychitty.com